O

£3

D1615641

Ritual Murder

Ritual Murder
Essays on liturgical reform

edited by BRIAN MORRIS

Carcanet Press · Manchester

SBN 85635 2950
First published in 1980 by
Carcanet New Press Limited
330 Corn Exchange Buildings
Manchester M4 3BG

Typeset by Input Typesetting Ltd
Printed in Great Britain by
Billing & Sons Ltd, Guildford, London and Worcester

Contents

Introduction   BRIAN MORRIS   7

A plea for our Common Prayer   DAVID MARTIN   11

The Book of Common Prayer as a repository of
    doctrine   GORDON TAYLOR   32

Shakespeare and the Prayer Book   A. L. ROWSE   47

Liturgy and literature   BRIAN MORRIS   58

The new religious English   ANDOR GOMME   75

A poesis of recurrence   J. P. WARD   100

Texts and contexts   FRASER STEEL   117

A friendly view   PEGGY MAKINS   124

Faith and song   SYDNEY CARTER   134

A college sermon   BRYAN THWAITES   140

Stewardship in the great tradition
    PETER NEWMAN BROOKS   148

The other liturgical revolution   I. R. THOMPSON   154

Notes on the contributors   165

Acknowledgments   168

Introduction
BRIAN MORRIS

This book is born out of a sense of crisis and concern. The decision by the General Synod of the Church of England to introduce a book of Alternative Services in 1980 has focussed public attention on the process of biblical and liturgical revision that has been going on, steadily and painstakingly, for decades; it extends across denominational, national and linguistic boundaries, and it could accurately be described as a most significant development in contemporary Christianity.

The impulse towards new translation and liturgical revision is a good and wholesome thing. But it is pointless and perilous to accept the results of such an impulse without stringent scrutiny and critical evaluation. The New English Bible, the Jerusalem Bible, the Good News Bible, the vernacular versions of the Roman Catholic Mass, and the Anglican Series 2 and 3 services are all products of this drive to 'make it new', and they have been examined, from time to time, by Christians of all kinds. Many of those Christians have reported shock, distress and profound dissatisfaction at what they have discovered. The 'new' mutations are considered by many people to be, in many respects, doctrinally strange and linguistically distasteful – completely unacceptable as anything except experiment. The present very real danger is that these experiments, with all their imperfections on their heads, will become the accepted texts of the scriptures and the liturgy, and, worse still, the *only* versions available to future generations. Within a matter of a few years from today English Christians may well find those matchless masterpieces, the Authorised Version of the Bible and the Book of Common Prayer, banished from the pew, the pulpit, the lectern and the altar, and relegated to the museum and the library as outmoded survivors of a bygone age. Their places may easily be taken by these 'new' versions, on the grounds that they are more 'relevant' and more likely to attract the young. There is not one atom of evidence for either claim.

We contend that to discard them would be disastrous. It would be a failure of faith, of taste, and of nerve. The various international bodies like ICET and the International Commission on English in the Liturgy (ICEL), and above all the Anglican Liturgical Commission, have produced nothing worthy to replace, as standard texts for public worship and private meditation, the great originals they have attempted to revise. Nor could they possibly have done so. In its present state of development and flux the English language is simply not capable of rendering the great truths of the Christian faith in words and rhythms that are both contemporary and profound. The poet C. H. Sisson summed it up when he said, 'There is no such thing as passing on profound truths in superficial speech.' It would require a genius of the stature of Wyclif, Coverdale or Cranmer to attempt the task of revision and unfortunately genius does not come to order. It cannot be whistled down out of the heavens by an international committee or a liturgical commission.

We are not against progress; we are in no way contemptuous of change. The 'new' versions of our bewildered and fractured age have many things to offer; they contain many insights and occasional felicities; they are entirely suitable as adjuncts and accessories to worship and devotion. But they must never be allowed to usurp the place of books like the Authorised Version and the Book of Common Prayer as the central, accepted and authoritative texts for the Church's public worship. As Peter Newman Brooks says, 'the Great Tradition' must be preserved.

The contributors to this volume of essays constitute an important and wide cross-section of contemporary Christian opinion in this country. There is no clique or pressure-group here. They include Anglicans, non-Anglicans, and a Member of the Society of Friends. Their expertise covers such fields as Elizabethan history, journalism, literary criticism, counselling, pastoral theology, naval history, sociology, mathematics and music; there are some poets, some priests, some professors. There has been no formal examination of their religious 'credentials', but probably all would 'profess and call themselves Christians' of one sort or another. I invited them to give their personal views on the present state of liturgical and biblical revision, and to comment on the significance to themselves of the great translations of the past which are currently under threat. There are two exceptions: I have included Bryan Thwaites's 'A College Sermon' and Peter Newman Brooks's 'Stewardship in the Great Tradition' although they were not specifically commissioned for this book. The authors have kindly consented to be included, and their presence emphasises how wide and deep is the concern for these great issues.

It must be stressed that no 'party line' was laid down, and (so far as I know) no consultation has taken place between any of the various contributors. But a remarkable degree of unanimity, and even perhaps of repetition, has emerged. All of us love and reverence the work of Cranmer and his contemporaries; all of us believe it to be profoundly relevant to present-day Christianity; all of us know it to be in danger.

We all hope that these essays will reach the widest possible public, and we trust that they will inform and encourage Christian readers, stimulating them to become actively, vigorously, involved in the vital task of preservation. This, indeed, is the acceptable hour: now is the time for all good men to come to the aid of our priceless, irreplaceable inheritance of liturgy, literature and worship. For 'be ye well assured' that unless those who care for our religious heritage are prepared to stand up, and speak up, and work to defend it, the time is at hand when it will be displaced. Then we shall find (for example) the Book of Common Prayer not in the church pew, but only in the vestry, the vicarage, the religious bookshop, or the British Library. St Paul spoke wisely to the Thessalonians when he advised them to 'prove all things', but he was even more judicious when he instructed them 'hold fast that which is good'.

A plea for our Common Prayer
DAVID MARTIN

Let me begin by pointing out something very odd and very obvious.

From 1549, the year when Cranmer first prepared the Book of Common Prayer, till 1949, most of our ancestors received little or no education and during that time Cranmer's little book was 'understanded of the people'. However, since 1949 a greater number of people have been educated, at ever increasing cost and to a progressively later age; at the same time there has been a continuing revolution in methods which are designed to enrich our sensibilities and to extend our cultural horizons. The result is that the little 'Book of Common Prayer' and that larger miracle, the Authorised Version of the Bible, together by universal consent the crown and glory of our language, are now declared 'difficult' and 'misleading'. Powerful voices claim that we are baffled and confused by the pure speech of our forebears. We are, they say, aliens to our past. The time has arrived to ditch our own treasures.

Meanwhile we are all apparently able to fill out income tax forms, and even to read the complicated leaflets which accompany them. We can follow television commentators who use the argot of sport, finance or pop music at fantastic speeds. We can even pick out the slovenly mouthings of film stars. But not, it seems, the Book of Common Prayer. A sentence like 'Man that is born of a woman hath but a short time to live' really taxes our understanding.

It is absurd, but people believe it. You hear people say just that kind of thing, as if it were the natural assumption of all sensible men. 'They' also say, with equal confidence, that relevance is the proper test of prayer, forgetting that today's relevance is tomorrow's obsolescence. Some things remain to be remembered.

Again, 'they' also say that the Book of Common Prayer is rude about human moral pretension, forcing us to turn to grace as a remedy for disgrace. Cranmer doesn't presuppose human niceness, even the niceness of English people assembled on a Sunday morning.

But as I write my daughter plays a record of rock music to this lyric: 'Now the leaves of sorrow turn their face/Scattered on the ashes of disgrace.' Notice those words: leaves, ashes, scatter, sorrow, turn. Every one of them is rooted deep in that supposedly lost world of Master Cranmer. Grace and disgrace we have always with us. It

11

is the century of Hiroshima, Auschwitz and Gulag Archipelago, and the intermittent grubbiness eating at all our lives. So how then is it 'irrelevant' to say 'The remembrance of them is grievous unto us, the burden of them is intolerable.'

We are also in a time when the therapists of the soul seek to uncover the malign diseases of our selfhood and absolve us from the burden and the taint. The psychotherapist takes a healing knife to a buried cancer, absolving and restoring those who truly seek restoration. Is it then so irrelevant to touch on the misery of our condition? Misery and mercy go together. The condition of misery evokes the quality of mercy, and this is because 'Thou art the same Lord, whose property is always to have mercy'.

That sentence containing the word 'property' brings us to one of the silliest aspects of liturgical chop and change: tiny alterations which trip up the tongue but do nothing to clarify the meaning. They have taken away the word 'property' in case you or I are tempted to misunderstand it. But how could we? It is an age of science in which we constantly talk of properties. Elements have properties, things that *belong* to them and pertain to them. It is also the age of advertisements for property. We know perfectly well that people have properties and that these *belong* to them. So property has to do with belonging. When we pronounce or hear that word 'property' in prayer we recollect that mercy belongs to God. It belongs to God to have mercy. It is an appropriate idea and we feel it right and proper, i.e., in the place where it *belongs*.

Let me remind you of another beautiful phrase also taken away: 'fulfilled with thy grace and heavenly benediction'. Like property the word 'fulfilment' is modern as well as ancient and we use it constantly. We seek fulfilment in work, and to be fulfilled in our home life and relationships. But what is pleasing about the prayer book version is that it invites men to be full of *benediction*. That interests us, because it is not quite what we expect. Benediction literally means 'good word'. A benediction is a last good word which brings us to a satisfying end. We are filled with benediction when we are finally satisfied with the goodness of the word.

Here then, in words like 'property' and 'fulfilled', we have little wells of meaning from which we can draw every time we pass. Sometimes we just pass by, but the well of meaning is always present – or was until just a short while ago.

Of course, in one sense these are small, unimportant examples. They occur in the revision called Series 2 which retains much of the meaning and rhythm of the old words. In Series 2 the itch for footling alteration was just beginning to assert itself. So we have to bear a nick here and a scratch there. The great arch of marvellous rime and reason remains. Yet the scratches still make us marvel that anybody should care to mar perfection. After all, a careless scratch in a record of Bach's 'Double Violin Concerto', is minute, but the carelessness cannot be ignored. Those who know and care about the arch of sound and reach into the well of meaning already sense the instinct for mindless damage which is at work. If a man is capable of messing about with great words in the English liturgy he could do it to Shakespeare. He could think himself competent to propose improvements on

> Shall I compare thee to a summer's day?
> Thou art more lovely and more temperate

It would perhaps be only a *little* alteration: a single word, a potent repetition. But imagine our indignation at the presumption of whoever attempted it.

This isn't a fiddling concern about words: it is anger that men should tamper with things so beautiful and so easily marred. We look after great pictures and have experts to restore them with care, knowledge and love. But in the church it seems we have 'experts' who damage rather than mend. These experts are equipped with a terrible talent for smoothing out the suggestive edge of meaning, for nicking the beat and the satisfying repetition. This is in part because they utilise versions put together by a Roman Catholic commission, ICEL,* centred in the USA, which tried to cater for

* This body is a shadowy organisation whose monopoly powers in the Roman Catholic Church have made it into a middle-sized corporation. It has worked within a rather restrictive rubric with a perverse philosophy of language and communication and a patronising attitude to those in reluctant receipt of its efforts. The attempt to cater for a large number of English-speaking contexts was bound to result in a much lower level of literary competence than is to be observed in the French, German and Spanish versions. Yet it is precisely the work of this body, in conjunction with its ugly sister, the International Consultation on English Texts, which has been fastened on the English Church. The beautiful Cinderella of our own liturgy has been banished in favour of this inelegant transatlantic sorority. Worse still, the ICEL cannot even get right the Latin text of its own Novus Ordo, and exercises a curious prejudice against words like 'Sanctus' and 'Beatus', as if holiness and blessedness were not quite nice or somehow unfashionable in advanced circles. The editor of *The Universe* claims to have discovered four hundred mistakes of commission and omission in its work. 'We believe' was taken up by this body in spite of the fact that the Novus Ordo retains 'Credo' and other linguistic groups continue to keep the first person. 'And also with you' was an unhappy invention of ICEL. 'Save us from the time of trial' was ICET work, passed by a small majority of the Commission, in which the crucial votes were American and Canadian. We need a new prayer in the Litany: 'from international bodies, from ICET, ICEL, and all their malignant inventions, good Lord deliver us.'

some two dozen different linguistic contexts from Fiji to Tipperary. It is also because they have not known how to draw on the reservoir of genius available to them. True, W. H. Auden was consulted but he made it clear that Coverdale could not be improved upon. T. S. Eliot attended some meetings in the very early stages and was apparently unable to speak a word. It was, if you like, a warning given by silence.

But a deeper reason lies in the fact that when the rationalising spirit takes over poetry is the first to suffer. Image and rhythm are thought of as decoration, mere adornment and verbal wrapping-paper. Yet poetry is far more than posies of pretty words arranged in pleasing patterns. Poetry is embodiment, the creator spirit incarnate, a mighty analogue of divinity and the soul in pilgrimage.

So far I've given quite minor instances of the capacity merely to fiddle without any contribution to clarity. Unfortunately, there are more major examples to hand; for instance, the Lord's Prayer. We have heard the Lord's Prayer since childhood, in school or from the lips of parents, and it is the deepest groove in our common prayer. We have only to recite it and we recognise *the* prayer which is held in common. This prayer is often called the family prayer, partly because it has been shared in our families, but also because it is almost the only prayer which is the shared possession of most people in the English-speaking family.

But if the work of the revisers has any effect at all it will destroy that common possession, separating church from church, church from school,* active churchman from occasional churchgoer, one part of the English family from another part, and – worst of all – parent from child. Any group invited to join in the Lord's Prayer will break into an uncertain babble of alternatives. Already there are multiple variants, as the revisers shuffle uncertainly from one version to another, utterly careless of the consequences. Congregations trip unhappily and helplessly from trespasses to debts to sins, only to end up with versions which are more obscure than the original.

What *does* 'do not bring us to the time of trial' mean? If the object is clarification then I for one admit mystification. The revisers do not even know themselves, because scholarly views differ, as indeed they always do. Prayer has become the sport of pedants, just as liturgy has become a kind of game for liturgiologists. What we have

* The Bishop of Bath and Wells, valiantly attempting at the July Synod (1979) to retain the Lord's Prayer, pointed out what a tiny minority of schools is influenced by the new ecclesiastical version.

in the multiple revisions of the Lord's Prayer is pedantry posing as modernity. It does not bring us together, even on the wider ecumenical front, because the Americans, for example, naturally and automatically say the old version, apart from the use of 'which' and 'them'. Thus the new versions achieve *just* enough change to confuse. They alter the habits of some churchpeople just sufficiently to separate them from other Christians and from English-speaking people at large. It is a malignant achievement, which unhinges one of our most precious shared possessions. The knowledge of Christian prayer is weak enough without being subject to confusion.

I conclude my introductory remarks by referring to something equally shocking, even though it affects fewer people.

So far I have underlined the creation of chaos, the footling character of some alterations, and the way pedantry poses as modernity and 'relevance'. However, one might suppose they would leave alone the collects at Matins and Evensong. Not even the greatest enthusiast for change can imagine that new people will be attracted by hollowing out the collects.

A collect enters the mind so powerfully because it has a particular sequence of thought realised in a miraculous balance of phrase. The collects in the Book of Common Prayer are small pattern prayers, tiny flights of intimate devotion:

Lighten our darkness we beseech thee O Lord . . .

O God who art the author of peace and lover of concord . . .

Yet these prayers have been as brutally mutilated as any statue hacked by fanatical troopers three hundred years ago. One can only contemplate such an act with stunned disbelief. If at any point we had supposed that the experts knew what they were up to then we were wrong. They know not what they do. The first aim of anyone who cares about our liturgy must be to restore the gutted interiors of the great collects and give beauty back to Matins and Evensong.

I write strongly, perhaps one may think, too strongly. So I quote now from what has been written by an agnostic, Lord Robbins; a Jew, Professor R. J. Werblowsky, and the Master of the Choristers, York Minster, Dr Francis Jackson. Lord Robbins modernised the structure of our higher education in the early 1960s, so he is no stranger to modernisation. This is what he has to say:

I find it difficult to describe in temperate language my feelings regarding the current tendency to reject the Jacobean translation of the Scriptures, to say nothing of the Book of Common Prayer, in favour of recent versions of these masterpieces.

Whether one is a believer or not, it is surely not open to question that, with Shakespeare, these works are the main background of our literary heritage. To substitute for their marvellous cadences and deep spiritual and poetic appeal, these supreme examples of literary insensibility aping on the sublime plane on which they move the dead-pan language of informal twentieth-century speech, seems to me an outrage which, if it were not a real danger, one would never believe to be possible.

Presumably the motive is well-intentioned – to make more 'real' the teaching, the narrative and the aspirations the sacred books and prayers embody. But this is a fallacy born of complete incomprehension of what 'tells' and what does not 'tell' in such communication with the young who after all are far more musical and just as sensitive to literary excellence as their predecessors. What would they – or we – say of an attempt to rewrite one of Hamlet's soliloquies in modern English? All eyes would be dry. How much more is to be condemned in this forcing the adoption of such parodies of the greatest literary manifestations of one of the great religions of the world.

Professor Werblowsky is one of the universal scholars of this generation, equally at home in Japanese religion, or in Thai Buddhism or Tunisian Islam. He writes:

Even outsiders and onlookers like myself have long been aware that the Anglican Church has embarked on a course similar to that taken by some other churches – with the big difference that the C of E has more to lose. Future students of Comparative Religion will write seminar papers on the total loss of sensibility in the Anglican Church, on the demise of the sense of what liturgy is about, and on the time-serving (mis)conceptions regarding what constitutes 'relevance'. I spend much time explaining to my students that the definition of today's relevance is tomorrow's antiquated irrelevance. Of course this obvious fact also has serious theological implications, e.g. the necessity that Holy Scriptures may have to be translated anew in every generation! But this holds true for purposes of 'reading', with the commentary included as it were in the reading of the text. Liturgical use is a different matter altogether. Of course most authors of sacred texts (except in cases of deliberate archaising) wrote the colloquial *koine* of their day. The big secret is that really great and inspired writing becomes 'classical' and remains so! Bach's fugues, though written in the musical colloquialisms of his day, are classical for ever. The same can be applied, *mutatis mutandis*, to religious and liturgical literary composition. The secret of liturgy (and of Scripture in liturgical use) is its ability to become classical, quite apart from the fact that liturgical language is always a language of quotations. The heaven is full of satellites, spaceships, and distant stars and galaxies – nothing else. When Christians speak of their Father which is in Heaven, they *quote* the language of their forebears who transmitted to them the faith. When will the C of E 'properly modernise' the Lord's Prayer? Perhaps also the Collect 'Stir up our hearts' should be amended to 'Give us a hang-up on you'.

I am puzzled about another feature of the current English insensitivity not only to liturgy but also to language. (Perhaps the two go together.) One of the unique features of the English 'Reformation' – i.e., of the history of the C of E – is the fact that it coincides with a climax in the history of English prose. Even the role of Luther's German in his reformation movement and in the subsequent cultural history of Germany provides no adequate analogy or comparison. The King James Bible, the BCP and what we today associate with the name of Cranmer are lasting monuments to this accidental (or providential?) conjunction. The degradation of language and liturgy seem to go hand in hand. It is no longer a matter of throwing out the baby with the bathwater but simply of throwing away a casket of jewels.

As a sociologist of religion I note that truly modern movements have a profounder awareness of the meaning of tradition. Trying to be with the 'in' thing or language, or catching up with the 'latest', is being neither modern nor relevant. I do not have to belabour the difference between a genuine 'reformation syndrome' and the spurious getting-ourselves-up-to-date obsession. It would be nice to be told one day that the C of E has come to its senses before it was too late.

Francis Jackson writes:

Last year in the cathedrals of Australia I was interested to witness the widespread dismay at the imposition of the new prayer book – apparently against the wishes of some worshippers . . . It would appear that the worshipper has done all in his or her power to give the new liturgies a fair hearing, and I think there is now a strong reaction as they compare the new with the old and see what is at stake.

George Steiner makes the same point very simply: 'England is losing the tongue which was the pulse of her being.'

Having said something about *what* has been done I should now say something about *how* these things have been managed and what sort of reasons have been offered. The manner of liturgical change is little less disturbing than the matter.

Until quite recently few people noticed that the Book of Common Prayer was being quietly installed in a museum for lost rites. Most Anglicans laboured under the reasonable presumption that somebody, somewhere, knew what he was about. A period of 'experiment' had been declared and no rash innovation appeared finally installed as a permanent fixture. In any case, the changes were mostly on an instalment plan, so that protest only flared intermittently. The familiar scenery was not just trundled away overnight, though individual churches often switched quite suddenly. An Anglican unable to find the Book of Common Prayer at his own church, or even in his own area, might suppose he was just unlucky or badly served. The experimenters had clearly decided 'gently does it'. At least that is how they started, though more recently caution has been replaced by zeal and haste. Perhaps they didn't initially know where they were going themselves, and then shed opposition as they went ahead. It is reliably reported that Archbishop Ramsey anticipated no such change as has now occurred.

The initial acquiescence is understandable. Some of us have acquiesced for years, not wanting to cause a fuss and in any case not wanting to believe what was almost staring us in the face. The clergy of the English Church are, after all, well known for pardonable pride in its liturgy, and are decent guardians of our national treasures. It is not like them to push people from pillar to porch. Persistent complaints about imposition without consultation, or about the manipulation of parish councils, or else about the long hierarchy of gearings all the way from people to parochial council to deanery to general synod, seemed a bit exaggerated. Warning letters to *The Times* from the Bishop of Chester and others went unheeded.

Even those who suspected the 'experiment' was really intended as a permanent imposition diligently examined themselves for signs of irrational nostalgia. There are places where you can find lively congregations using the new forms and nobody wants to depreciate such excellent and devoted work. It is very unlikely that these congregations are lively *because* of Series 3 but it seems ungracious to point this out too harshly. Any kind of impact in modern society seems worth a sympathetic hearing and appraisal. Even when one knows that the recent years of experiment have been mostly years of recession (especially so in the American Episcopal Church, where membership has dropped by nearly one third) still one exercises charity and caution, almost indeed until it is too late. Could it be that those of us who are disturbed put their personal preferences before zeal for mission? Might we have become fuddy-duddies overnight? These have been proper and decent questions for people to ask themselves.

After all in many parishes, perhaps most, you could still find the historic liturgy at off-peak hours, say at eight o'clock, and the elderly were allowed to pick up their crumbs midweek. When the matter was discussed in the House of Lords in March 1978 one noble lord had a simple solution worthy of Marie Antoinette: Let them travel by car. 'This is the age of the car', he said. Other members of the House reminded him that some people actually *belonged* to churches, had become attached to them, and had lived lovingly and companionably with the old rite for many years. Edward Short pointed out that nowadays 'Anything can happen anywhere'. Lord Sudeley made an eloquent plea for a wider range of proper consultation. Clearly there was widespread concern on all sides.

The trouble is that many people are thoroughly unused to debate in the church. To them the church offers services, above all, a service. It takes a little while to recognise that the Church could become the kind of organisation where you may have to badger your local official or argue your case in public if you are not to be overlooked and discounted. Up to now the Church of England has not been like the kind of industry which shuts down services unless there is a local rumpus. People who love the Prayer Book are not inclined to cause trouble, divide a small community, berate the vicar, lobby the PCC. They are reluctant even to recognise that this is now forced upon them. One noble lord actually said that people who don't stand up to their vicars deserve what they get. Still they are unwilling to conclude that the church is changing its style as well as its liturgy. That change is almost as sad as the loss of the great words, because we are forced to 'speak now or else for ever hold our peace'. There is now almost the aura of the kind of trade union where democracy is the will of the vocal and where you need to 'participate' frantically just to prevent caucuses pushing their views.

Quiet people feel unable to say anything and retire in horrified silence, or else they keep their reluctant acquiescence to themselves. They are told – wrongly I believe – that this is a necessary sacrifice for the sake of the new generation. Some of the older generation feel their age makes their opinions invalid. Perhaps they hope the next generation will like the new just as they liked the old. Maybe liking is just a matter of pleasant and happy associations. You just have to get used to it, like putting up with the new glass and plastic monster they've erected in what was once a comely town. Those who don't and won't conform are just stuck in their ways, irreconcilables.

Our contemporary democracy has too often become 'the will of the vocal' and the power of the caucus. Yet it was the democratic argument which muted some complaints, because bishops in particular were inclined to argue this was the 'will of the people'. There was another argument used in good faith, which ran like this. Dr David Frost, for example, back in 1975 wrote that there was no question of people being deprived of the Book of Common Prayer. This, of course, is no longer true only four years later. Vicars write to church papers to say that it is available at eight o'clock, so everybody is satisfied. Other people do not see the implications of this, and argue that Cranmer will remain just as Shakespeare remains. But Shakespeare is taught in schools, and his language is made available. No school decrees that those with an old-fashioned taste for Shakespeare can indulge it if they like to turn up at unsocial hours.

This is an important point, because not only is the Book of Common Prayer not available at all in some churches and some areas, but the less extreme measures just as surely decree it will be practically extinct in twenty years. So it is not a question of each man to his taste or of allowing variation, and experimental alternatives. *It is straightforwardly and without any doubt a matter of survival.* We have to make up our minds *now* whether we are ready to put Cranmer on the dust heap of history, or take firm measures to ensure that his little book is made available. If the younger generation is not allowed to know it then the younger generation has been deprived of the right to choose it.

Let me explain, because this really is crucial. If the historic liturgy is only available at eight o'clock, or worse still mid-week, it immediately becomes the property of a diminishing enclave, not the shared treasure of the church. This tendency is reinforced because great emphasis is placed on Sunday mid-morning celebrations. Mid-morning is the natural time for young people, and many who prefer the Book of Common Prayer nevertheless come at that time because it is the family service with an atmosphere designed for children and with additional opportunities for sociability. Moreover, the current eucharistic emphasis positively denigrates Matins and Evensong, quite apart from turning even these services over to Series 3, and depriving those loyal to the old liturgy even in their last refuge. Unless the Book of Common Prayer retains an honoured place at principal services it is bound to disappear. What is not known cannot be chosen.

The revisers are well aware of this and perhaps realise that ignorance can effectively deprive the young of any option but their own liturgical essays and compositions. Thus they monopolise confirmation classes and endeavour to bring confirmands up entirely under the influence of the productions of the Liturgical Commission and the ICET. The same process occurs in many theological colleges, where Series 3 is constantly pushed at the expense of Cranmer. In the course of speaking at many theological colleges over the past three or four years I have never heard the old liturgy, even at Evensong! The new clergy are increasingly confirmands who have been kept from the happy infection of Cranmer and King James's Bible throughout their church life. In one famous college the students asked for the old liturgy to find out what it was like. If these decisions in the theological colleges are complemented (as they are) by the tendencies encouraged in the parishes then the future is clear and stark. In any other sphere you can imagine the cries of outrage if one party tried to subvert the younger generation entirely to its viewpoint, thereby isolating opposition.

It is all very odd because Anglicans have been tóld so often by their own leaders and by others that the prayerbook is the distinctive treasure of their Church. You have only to turn back to the celebrations of 1949 to see what they said then. The ordinary Anglican and many Englishmen with a deep affection for the church were glad to think that every day it entertained a quiet miracle. Robert Bridges, writing in 1913, spoke of the spires which stand up straight and tall 'for England'. Philip Larkin, not himself a believer, called the parish church 'a serious place on serious earth'. It was made so by accumulation, and by the repetition of these words.

What the great hymnbook of 1780 is to the Methodists and the Psalter is to the Presbyterians, the Book of Common Prayer is to the English Church: 'unique, unapproachable, elemental in its perfection'. With the Authorised Version it is our living link with ourselves and with the early modern phase of our language in its first simple and supple splendour. Herbert Howells, one of the finest of our church composers in the older generation, puts the threat quite simply: 'It is as if someone has gone around and put black marks on parish church after parish church, and one cathedral after another.'

So far something has been said about what has been done and how it has been done. But why?

One reason is to be found in the politics of ecumenical mergers. Many enthusiasts believe that the church is better organised in larger and larger agglomerates: the ecclesiastical equivalents of I.T.T. and the other multinationals. On the whole the ordinary Christian does not follow these negotiations and shows little interest in them. For example, research suggests that even the merger of Congregationalists and Presbyterians aroused very little interest among the members of those churches; it was pushed and pushed until exhaustion became acquiescence.

I am myself anxious for cooperation and charity between Christians, but I am troubled by the danger that all integrity will be lost and the distinctive character of varied traditions swallowed up in mere uniformity. This thrust to uniformity is certainly evident in the liturgical sphere. Thus, not only the Anglicans but the Methodists also have suffered suppression of the historic rite in the interests of versions devised in the ecclesiastical stratosphere. In particular the revisers have gone to the drawing-board with an eye on the Roman Catholic model. This is how we lost the mightily evocative 'Lord God of Hosts'. Some Roman reviser had imagined the peasantry might confuse 'hosts' with *the* host. So the English Church tamely followed suit, fearing to be different.

This would not in itself be so bad if the Roman Catholics themselves had not been so unlucky in the Englishing of the mass. As one eminent English bishop in the Roman Church said to me: 'We did it just at the wrong time.' The result, in the words of the Roman Catholic scholar Professor Denis Donoghue, is a liturgy which is 'just boring'. The Church of England was supremely lucky when it Englished the liturgy. W. H. Auden was right when he said 'Why spit on our luck?'

Many of these versions, whether they be of the Lord's Prayer, or the Creed or the Te Deum, are put together in international commissions with no feel for the genius of the English language or for what will wear liturgically. For example, the version of the Te Deum proposed by the ICET runs: 'You are God we praise you.' Comment is superfluous. The trendy 'we' inserted into the new Creed derives from precisely these international bodies. Again W. H. Auden was correct when he said he preferred to take personal responsibility for his beliefs. 'We believe' is like the use of the American 'hopefully', which dares not say 'I hope' but indicates impersonally that a certain amount of hoping is perhaps in order at the present juncture of the man-God dialogue.

I am not privy to the mechanics of these operations but one can easily guess how we come to be saddled with that repellent response 'And also with you', which to many people sounds like a *risqué* riposte in a radio or TV comedy. Ernie Wise would know exactly what to do with it.

The original phrase in Latin is *et cum spiritu tuo* and is translated 'and with thy spirit'. But perhaps the Catholics did not wish to choose a translation identical with that used in the Church of England and in a sorry moment chose 'And also with you'. (The other linguistic groups have been more lucky: *Et avec votre esprit; Und mit deinem Geist; E con il tuo spirito.*) And then, amazingly, the Church of England followed suit. The Anglican revisers were perhaps hoping finally to rid themselves of that dangerous word 'spirit'. 'Spirit' seemed to them not quite modern, though they preferred it to 'ghost'. They feared the laity might suppose the priest *had* a spirit, like some genie called up in a bottle, or even that he kept a flask of spirit tucked up his surplice. So they went through the texts turning 'ghost' into 'spirit' and trying to exorcise spirit as often as possible. They got rid of the spirit and exorcised the beauty.

The next reason, aside from high level ecclesiastical politics, has to do with the assumed capacities of the younger generation and the supposed requirements and demands of modern communication. There is little doubt that many clergymen deeply attached to the English liturgy have reluctantly abandoned it because they have been persuaded it does not come over to 'modern' people. Nobody has quite explained how gutting and gouging the collects and putting the Creed in the first person plural is going to attract the young away from cars and TV, but there are doubtless some who think such shifts will have an impact.

In fact there is no evidence whatever that the decline of attendance and participation has anything to do with the language used in divine worship. Indeed, the period of experimentation happens to have been a period in which participation has fallen further. We do at least know that some people no longer desire to attend church precisely because they have been deprived of the old rite.

This is not a matter on which it is easy or proper to dogmatise, but the overwhelming weight of evidence suggests that the factors bringing about lower participation are to be found in certain features of modern society, not in language. These factors have to do with the break-up of primary communities, the shift from active to passive participation in most forms of voluntary activity, rival attractions and varied facilities for leisure, including television, the car and the disco. These are not exhaustive, but there is much sociological material on these matters, some of it complicated. In the course of reading hundreds of books and articles on the subject I have not found one which attributes weakening impact to the presence of great language. Perhaps people like to think that language is to blame because then the problem seems easily dealt with. Thus the liturgy becomes the scapegoat for processes arising from the structural dynamics of modern society. Nobody asks why it is that the specialised 'registers' used in auctioning or in pop festivals or sports are so easily absorbed, even though they have no more affinity with so-called 'ordinary everyday language' than Cranmerian English. They too have a character, a specific context and purpose. The right way to speak today depends on context. Mrs Thatcher delivering a speech to the Conservative Party Conference does not speak like a Billingsgate porter slipping on a wet fish.

This question of 'appropriate character' is linked to another reason put forward in defence of what has happened. It is suggested that religion should be in everyday language or the language of the market place. Now, those who glibly refer to 'everyday language' do not really mean what they say. Everyday English is very varied and bound to local context. It is what you hear at a match in Chelsea or in a Manchester pub. This is how people speak, and liturgy cannot be translated into it without unimaginable transformation and localised fragmentation. Only in this way, however, could it hope to cross the barrier between the various forms of standard English, whether of this or the seventeenth century, and the everyday speech of the people. So what the revisers have in mind is the bloodless variant of modern English deployed, for example, when people stand up on platforms and stick to the 'official' rules of contemporary grammar. But this style is instantly recognised as associated with officialese, and is no more accepted as 'natural' by the bulk of Englishmen than any English used in the past. It is specific to certain occasions and to the educated when on their best grammatical behaviour.

Moreover, this style is now under pressure and is changing rapidly. Any attempt to use it for liturgical purposes either ensures obsolescence within a generation, or the same disruptive and impoverishing exercise has to be undertaken in 1995. Our official speech of today will then seem like a cast-off linguistic garment, while the classic liturgy remains as available as ever. Nothing ages as rapidly as yesterday. And the odd thing is that some revisers recognise this and speak of a form to last us fifteen years or for the rest of the century. In short, they offer us expendable liturgy: the erosion of cumulative power and meaning by successive revisions. This in turn means that the potency of liturgy is destroyed, because cumulation, quotation, and repetition are the heart of evocation and invocation.

So the argument based on the supposed need for 'everyday' English is absurd, because the very idea is impossible. You cannot put the speech of the divine office in the lingo of the everyday office. The Stock Exchange will not serve any more than Billingsgate or the style of a circular from the town hall. The 'market place' doesn't exist. *Nobody* speaks like Series 3. It is a very odd market indeed where they say 'God from God' and ask to be saved from 'the time of trial'.*

Even in 1662 the English of public prayer was not the style used by Pepys in his diary. When the loiterers watched another head stuck on Temple Bar or the whores exchanged ribaldries by Charing Cross they didn't do so in Cranmerian prose. But they did at least know that everything is after its kind: crabbed grammar in legal affairs, elegant foppery or country matters on the stage. Cranmer himself never attempted everyday speech, only speech which was understandable. And the AV itself was written from the first in deliberately archaic language.

What about the hymns? It is sad to realise that whereas the average hymn used to be the weakest part of a service, it is now often the strongest. People turn with visible and audible relief to the strong language of a great hymn. A mighty chant like 'O God our help in ages past' is just as distant in language and just as powerful and simple in effect as the words of Cranmer. Indeed, English hymnody is saturated in cross-references and quotations which rest on the traditional language of the church, above all the Authorised Version. If the argument against the liturgy and the Authorised Version were correct then we would have to give up hymns and traditional words together. You cannot admit that congregations enjoy singing Wesley and Watts and simultaneously argue that Cranmer is beyond our comprehension.

And it is as inconsistent to maintain the traditional vestments as it is to sing the traditional hymns! You would expect the apologists of relevance to abolish the clothes and the prose at the same time.

* Perhaps I should mention that the Book of Common Prayer is closer to western and northern dialect than is standard English. Think on't, in case tha's not thowt on't before. What's the matter with thee, lad?

Likewise the bells and the candles. Yet few people have taken up Derek Brewer's sardonic suggestion that the candles at baptism should be replaced by battery torches.

Before we explore what can be done and what has to be done it is good to remind ourselves of the loss which faces us. Basil Wiley, a Methodist and himself a consultant for the New English Bible, felt that the historic liturgy was 'the poetry of the church', uniquely capable of putting us 'in touch with all traditional feeling'. This approach to liturgy doesn't think in terms of archaic and modern, but in terms of cumulation, and of historic resources which can be continually tapped. Thus the range of meaning is extended by a communion between past and present and future: 'future and past subsisting now' as Charles Wesley put it. Once the life-blood of language is thinned then piety loses body and weight. It is difficult to convey this sense of weight and accumulation but the believer who takes on his lips the common prayer becomes truly catholic and inclusive, placing himself in a great chain of meaning. Take some of the most miraculous lines in English. 'He came all so still/There his mother was/As dew in April/That falleth on the grass'. That is far older than the prayerbook, but it is also dateless. Form and meaning are fused and both speak across centuries through the medium of verbal music. You must not mangle the music. Alter the medium and you destroy or cripple the message. Quiet simple words and simple, quiet meaning belong together.

The pulse of meaning is conveyed in rhythm and movement: in the beat if you like. The sound of English prayer moves forward. That is why it moves *people*. Speaking of Dante Steiner describes how with each ascent from sphere to sphere 'language is submitted to more intense and exact pressure of vision . . . we hear the prayer in the syntax.' This is what Shakespeare might call 'form and pressure'. It gives vitality. Steiner asks us to 'Compare the vitality of language implicit in Shakespeare, in the Book of Common Prayer, or in the style of a country gentleman such as Cavendish, with our present vulgate.'

It is these words which can carry the freight of joy or sorrow, and are framed to the occasion, whether to marriage or burial, to pleading or glorifying. Listen to the words which carry the heaviest freight of all:

Man that is born of a woman hath but a short time to live.

Suffer us not, at our last hour, for any pains of death, to fall from Thee.

And now, Lord, what is my hope: truly my hope is even in Thee.

There is no ordinary everyday language which can serve that occasion. Yet the words of the burial service are the simplest we have. There are only four of more than one syllable in three sentences. The music of the words is no ordinary music, but it is composed of the simplest materials.

Once you lose touch with those rhythms you lose touch with the historic grounding of religion and a layer of response deep in bone, marrow and tissue. We are creatures of rhythm and movement. If you go to a Pentecostal meeting you see the rhythmic raising of the hands, you feel the powerful pressure of great words and remembered scriptures, and you experience the movement of the Spirit. And who, incidentally, understands speaking with tongues? Only those to whom understanding is given, and there's plenty of room for misunderstanding. Yet the communication is powerful because there is a movement of the spirit. Cut out the rhythm and you destroy the movement.

We understand through movement and we understand across centuries. But what is understanding? To understand is to get caught up in the spirit of the thing, joining in the movement. I don't happen to be charismatically inclined but I don't mind if people do. It so happens that our English liturgy contains a quiet invitation to the movement of the spirit couched in some of the most powerful syllables we possess. Once you have caught on then a tiny misunderstanding here or there doesn't matter a jot. You need to learn how to join in of course, just as you have to pick up the lingo of pop or the argot of costermongers. Nothing is absolutely natural and normal. But the barriers are tiny and the rewards enormous. True, we don't say as we turn over in bed or pass the marmalade: 'My soul doth magnify the Lord/And my spirit hath rejoiced in God my saviour.' But so what? There is a time to pass the marmalade and a time to use great words. The modern meaning of 'magnify' actually increases the pleasure and profit in using it. In science you use a lens to concentrate vision. So to magnify the Lord is to concentrate your vision. And the force of 'magnify' is exactly the force of 'property': a word deployed in science utilised also in the vocabulary of faith.

This is another aspect of the loss facing us: the hint of something extra and other which allows constant repetition. In most great works there is an exciting mixture of simplicity and nuggets of half-apprehended meaning. There's usually a brown nut of sense waiting for you to chew over. My son is reading *The Sword and the Stone* by T. H. White and has become fascinated by the word 'sward'. Was it a funny spelling of sword? The uncertainty tickled him till he found out. A tiny variation or extension of meaning incites curiosity and invites explanation. The author pronounced a very special curse on whoever whittled the meaning down.

An occasional oddity eggs us on to comprehension. For example, there is the phrase 'By thy special grace preventing us'. Prevent means 'go before'. Grace then is what goes before. It is a mixture of protection and anticipation. Immediately Cranmer has turned you on to a fascinating idea which is also technical theology. Grace goes before you all your days. Or to put it in the language of theology: we are subject to prevenient grace.

Let me now quote at length from Psalm 107 in the Prayer Book version as translated by Miles Coverdale.

> They that go down to the sea in ships: and occupy their business in great waters;
> These men see the works of the Lord: and his wonders in the deep.
> For at his word the stormy wind ariseth: which lifteth up the waves thereof,
> They are carried up to the heaven, and down again to the deep: their soul melteth away because of the trouble.
> They reel to and fro, and stagger like a drunken man: and are at their wit's end.
> So when they cry unto the Lord in their trouble: he delivereth them out of their distress.
> For he maketh the storm to cease: so that the waves thereof are still.
> Then are they glad, because they are at rest: and so he bringeth them unto the haven where they would be.

That is powerful stuff. Generations of islanders brought up on no more than dame school learning have been caught in that enormous wave of words. Fishermen, masthead boys and merchants have known what it is to 'do business in great waters'. Those words are the sound of England.

For believers they are also an anchor for faith. Every now and then the bark of Christ shifts and shudders. In the early years of the eighteenth century, for example, God appeared to have become as mechanical and remote as the Newtonian universe, far removed from embodiment in human kind. And human beings appeared rational and reasonable, far removed from the profound mischief of sin. But the church was anchored in enormous words and powerful syllables proclaiming the embodiment of God and the redemption of man.

What *is* to be done? We have a case to make which we must repeat over and over again till the General Synod responds and the bishops put their voices where assuredly their hearts *must* be.

First, our English common prayer is simple and direct.

Second, next to nobody will be brought in by the adoption of speech-day or platform English and many will go sadly away. A weak variant of standard English crosses none of the barriers of contemporary society.

Third, there is anyway no such thing as a universal modern English into which common prayer may be translated.

Fourth, English today is in a fluid condition, and once you embark on this exercise you are committed to repeating it over and over again. The confusions will be great; and there will be no prayer which is shared and common. The novel will rapidly be more out of date than the old, like yesterday's fashion. Nothing ages like novelty.

Fifth, nothing is gained by a mangled echo of the past. Are we really incapable of making something new to place *alongside* what we have? Is it necessary to chip and hollow out perfection?

Sixth, nothing should be done to disendow those loyal to the English liturgy, or treat them as second-class citizens indulged at off-peak hours. Common prayer should be available for those who desire it, in their local churches for at least some main services. This was recommended in the Guide to Parishes (1975) issued under the authority of the standing Sub-Committee of Synod. *Everybody* should have the opportunity to know it.

Seventh, this is English and therefore *ours*. We ought to retain access to the highest achievements of our language. Above all, we ought to retain access to the potent range of meanings opened up in the first youth of the English tongue. This means the regular reading of the Authorised Version as well as regular use of the Book of Common Prayer. The AV is the great vehicle for the public use of Scripture and should be used as the classic translation in English. Other versions should be used as occasion suggests: for incidental clarification maybe or because from time to time they are felicitous in the rendering of particular passages.

The opportunity to know and the right to exercise an option depend on universal availability. Unless young people in confirmation classes hear the historic liturgy regularly and unless it is in normal use in theological colleges it will die of attrition. The Book of Common Prayer has to be a universal, shared possession. This does not mean stopping experiment or ceasing to explore alternatives. But it does mean careful measures to ensure that Cranmer's liturgy is not subtly elbowed out or mutilated by successive revision. Prayer should be common, i.e. shared. And the Book of Common Prayer is something to be shared between ourselves now, and between the past and the future.

All I can say is that with age I find myself enjoying more and more the words and rhythms of the Book of Common Prayer. Apart from their meaning, they *sound* right and they are not talking down to us by being matey, and where they're a bit vague and archaic, that makes them grand and historic. The words give me time to meditate and pray; they are so familiar, they are like my birthplace, and I don't want them pulled down.

We are all of us preservationists who have had the luck to come out of the womb alive and with all our faculties.

SIR JOHN BETJEMAN

The Book of Common Prayer as a repository of doctrine

GORDON TAYLOR

Amid all the intellectual conflicts of the twentieth century, including especially the bitter debate about Education, it is vital that a Christian can explain in some measure the nature of his belief. Unless Christianity can express its convictions by showing them to be reasonable it cannot survive, and should not expect to do so. No progress towards the reconversion of England can be made until the teaching office of the church is so strengthened that clergy *and laity* both know what they believe and how they can best commend it to others.

Since we wish to be both rational and Christian we must have a theology; and therefore Christian theology, the science of our religion, is a necessity. The purpose of Christian theology is to explain the truth about God and his dealings with mankind, as these have been revealed in history. Christian doctrine is merely Christian teaching, and its dogmas are specific items in that doctrine which have become primary assumptions implicit in Christian life and experience. Simple instances of dogmas are the Fatherhood of God, the Divinity of Christ and the Godhead of the Holy Ghost.

Like all knowledge, Christian theology is based on experience. The dogma has always had to fit the facts, not the facts the dogma as some who are unversed in Christianity might imagine. The facts are chiefly to be found in Holy Scripture, and particularly in the New Testament. For example, the Christian belief in the Holy Spirit is powerfully based on the references in the Epistles of St Paul to 'the Spirit', 'the Spirit of God' or 'the Holy Spirit', which, it must be assumed, were intelligible to the recipients of those epistles. Read with the picture drawn in the Acts of the Apostles of the life of the Christian community during the first few years of its existence, they appear to show that if the primitive Church believed in anything it believed in the Holy Spirit, and was conscious of its power in their lives. Thus the emergent belief of that community in the Holy Spirit fitted its personal experience, and eventually became expressed in the Creeds which have come down to us. It follows that Christianity must ever have a strong appeal to antiquity, which establishes a continuity between the teaching and order of the Church today and the teaching and order of the early Church. If we are tempted to abandon that appeal to antiquity we should frankly and honestly admit that we are founding a new Christianity and abandoning the traditional kind.

Of course, in accordance with the promise of Jesus that the Holy Spirit would guide us into all truth, the continuing experience of the Church will involve the gaining of new insights which will be added to the sum-total of Christian experience. This is inevitable because in many directions in recent years there have appeared complex moral situations which were unknown to our forefathers. We must not act, or teach, as if the whole of Truth was given only to the Christians of nearly two thousand years ago. Perhaps our failure to appreciate this has been a limiting factor in the Church's progress during this twentieth century, and if we had realised the difficulty sooner we should not have had to deal with such a wholesale reform as we are now seeing.

The Church's teaching of its doctrine must be centred on God rather than on man. In recent years we have been too ready to concentrate upon the needs of man rather than on the claims of God. It is man's bitter twentieth-century experience of war and inhumanity that has led to this error, and caused him to try to enthrone himself in the place of God, to the extent that man now questions whether God is of any value at all in the Universe which modern science has revealed. Yet it is only on a sound theology that the true doctrine of man can be rediscovered, for, though modern man may feel he has successfully usurped God's throne, nevertheless he knows in his heart that he is quite helpless in the Universe now revealed to him, and is merely the slave of the all-powerful state he has helped to create. As he wearies with the failure of every political change he embraces, and as he sees his God-given freedom continuously eroded by bureaucracy, he comes nearer to the inevitable realisation that it is the Christian doctrine of God, rather than secular philosophical theories about the nature of man, which will alone enable him to understand the meaning of his life.

With sound theology must go sound ethical teaching, for Christian doctrine and Christian morals cannot for long be separated. As the practice of the Christian faith has been steadily abandoned there has been a big deterioration in social and personal morality. There is now a large proportion of the population which fails to see the distinction between right and wrong, and which sometimes even accepts as right what the Christian Church condemns as wrong. In such a situation the Church must uncompromisingly declare that hatred, dishonesty, intemperance, pride, envy, falsehood and all the other sins are contrary to the law of God, and that such of these as are committed by the individual or the state are downright sins in God's sight.

It is beyond all doubt that Christian doctrine influences conduct, even residually through the medium of an ineradicable conscience when the dogmas themselves have been forgotten. When Christian doctrine first came under fire about a century ago its critics desired Christian morality to be preserved at all costs, for they wished to have their cake and eat it. The critics today, however, denigrate both doctrine and morality, without drawing a distinction between them, and require that any religion there is shall be vague and comfortable, and practised without spiritual discipline of any kind.

What has upheld both doctrine and morality for members of the Church of England for the past four hundred years and has prevented their religion from becoming vague and comfortable is our Prayer Book, which first saw the light of day in 1549 and was amended in 1552 and 1662. For the layman especially it provided the only spiritual discipline he experienced. Copies of it were in most homes, even if the books were rarely read privately, and they were always on hand for reference when needed. In a host of ways the Prayer Book is the repository of doctrine for the common man. The Apostles' Creed in both Morning and Evening Prayer, the Nicene Creed in the Communion service and the Athanasian Creed following Evening Prayer of course spell out the doctrine particularly, but it is also present by implication throughout the book. The Thirty-Nine Articles often placed at the end have as their express purpose 'the Avoiding of Diversities of Opinions, and for the Establishing of Consent touching True Religion'. The Church of England (Worship and Doctrine) Measure of 1974 made permanent the temporary powers which the Church of England had been granted by Parliament in 1965 to authorise the use of other forms of service than those prescribed in the Prayer Book of 1662. At first it was presumed that the Measure would not only give to the Church of England the freedom to govern its own doctrine and worship but also (and in particular) to revise the Book of Common Prayer; this, however, was quickly denied in the public press by the Bishop of London, who pointed out that such revision could not be achieved except by recourse to Parliament under existing procedures. He went on to say that only an Act of Parliament or a General Synod Measure, both of which would require affirmative resolutions in both Houses, could in future cause the Prayer Book to be revised.

The Church of England (Worship and Doctrine) Measure of 1974 took effect on 1 September 1975. It states:

1 (1) It shall be lawful for the General Synod
  (a) to make provision by Canon with respect to worship in the Church of England, including provision for empowering the General Synod to approve, amend, continue or discontinue forms of service;
  (b) to make provision by Canon or regulations made thereunder for any matter, except the publication of banns of matrimony, to which any of the rubrics contained in the Book of Common Prayer relate;

but the powers of the General Synod under this subsection shall be so exercised as to ensure that the forms of service contained in the Book of Common Prayer continue to be available for use in the Church of England.

Thus it is clear that the General Synod was given no power to revise the Book of Common Prayer by Canon (as opposed to Measure) and without reference to Parliament, and therefore that in such respect the situation is little different from that which prevailed at the time of the attempted revision in 1927–8 when Acts of Parliament were required and failed. However, there is no guarantee that some future General Synod cannot or will not attempt to revise the Prayer Book by Measure in the manner allowed, relying on a disaffected or hostile Parliament to offer no opposition and to wash its hands like Pontius Pilate while saying 'See ye to it'. What can happen in the future is anyone's guess, and perhaps all that can be said is that the Prayer Book may be safe from revision for possibly another fifty years. Recent bitter public experience may prove to be its greatest safeguard. The unchanging situation about the Prayer Book appears to be as Archbishop Randall Davidson described it when he resigned in 1928: 'The majority of churchmen want no change. But the people who do want the change are the people who have studied the subject'. To that comment he added 'and care about it most'. That, however, is not true today. Those who care about the Prayer Book most want no change at all: the advocates of change care nothing at all about the Prayer Book and wish to remove it altogether from the scene, so that they can get on with founding a new Church.

It was inevitable that those inside the Church and outside it who wished to sponsor the new morality would see that a major obstacle in the way of their purposes was the Book of Common Prayer, because it was clearly too scriptural, too fair and open and too comprehensive to permit their intrigues. One of the Book of Common Prayer's proclaimed main endeavours was to enable the people to hear 'God's most holy word' according to an orderly plan. Another was to ensure that the congregation could both hear and join in the services, the minister being frequently enjoined to speak 'in a loud voice'. Yet another was to combine the finest traditions of Hebrew song, the Greek Fathers and the medieval Latin services, whilst adding or adapting the services being used in the sixteenth century by the Continental reformers. This was specially true of the Communion service, in which the devotions of many Churches were assembled round the central words of Christ spoken 'in the same night that he was betrayed'.

In addition to all this, the Book of Common Prayer was even more comprehensive in that it was drawn up so as to include different religious opinions, with a most exemplary charity which puts to shame the vengeful spirit of those who ensured its shelving in 1974 and the manner in which they worked. The Prayer Book tried most bravely to be both Catholic and Reformed, in the realisation of the nature of those whom it sought to unite, and to keep them in the same Church. Unfortunately it failed in its noble design, but the charitable and statesmanlike attempt it made left a permanent mark upon the Church of England. In a particularly perceptive moment Professor G. M. Trevelyan wrote in his *History of England*:

> Cranmer's revived Prayer Book was the golden mean. It served well on board Drake's ships before and after battle with the idolaters . . . yet the concealed Catholic, doubtfully attending church to avoid the twelve-penny fine, was often less shocked than he feared, and could remind himself that these were still the old prayers, though in English. The book was a chameleon which could mean different things to different people.

Since many Englishmen of the time of Queen Elizabeth I were, like her, children of the Renaissance rather than the Reformation, the Book of Common Prayer of 1552 had of necessity to be of such a kind as Trevelyan described. For the unchanging Englishman, unattracted by the pursuit of truth for truth's sake, bored by philosophy and addicted to mental sloth, yet passionately desiring that every dog should have his day, it could not possibly be otherwise. It was consensus, compromise, reconciliation, adaptability and reparation all rolled into one, the whole being done, not for the Church's sake, but for the sake of God and the Gospel. Every Pelagian Englishman, desiring only peace after long ecclesiastical strife, and preoccupied by the freedom conferred upon him by the

Renaissance and his dreams of the new worlds beyond the seas, could lay to heart whatever in its contents he chose. In a strange way it was still an age of faith, and that is possibly why such generosity prevailed. The liturgical upheaval of the present time takes place in an age when too many of its activists have long ago lost the faith of their fathers, and when the common Englishman, having already decided that Church membership is not for him, is either unaware of what has transpired, or, if he is aware, is totally uninterested.

Cries for liberty always seem to produce merely new masters, for, as Dr Johnson observed, 'They who most loudly clamour for liberty do not most liberally grant it.' So it is not surprising to find that the General Synod is in fact an oligarchy which is not directly elected by the rank and file in the pews of the churches but by representatives of the representatives whom they elect to their church councils. The resulting situation resembles one which would arise if the election of Members of Parliament was not by the people generally but instead by their local authority councillors following local elections. Every three years the annual parochial meetings (theoretically of the rank and file in the pews) elect representatives to the Deanery Synods who in due course elect their representatives to the General Synod, such an arrangement alone being considered a manageable electorate. It is inevitable that such stratification opens up large opportunities to party pressure groups, who do not fail to seize them. The average parishioner and/or worshipper in his parish church therefore has no direct individual say in who represents him on the General Synod, and often little or no idea of what is done there in his name. As in the trade unions, the activists carry the day, though the members of the General Synod are no more than the representatives of the Deanery Synods who elect them. As democracy is defined as 'government by the people, direct or representative' it is clear that election to the General Synod cannot be considered democratic, since presumably that word does not envisage representation at more than one remove, in the normal way. What we now have, therefore, is a sham democracy slowly usurping the powers of the bishops of an episcopal church and changing it out of all recognition.

The oligarchy masquerading as a democracy which is the new and all-powerful General Synod, has grown up through muddled thinking, for synodical government should never be seen as an example of parliamentary democracy. The Church has never subscribed to the doctrine of *vox populi, vox Dei*. In an episcopal church, a synod is truly the bishop-in-council, who, like St James at Jerusalem, sums up the mind of the church on any matter and expresses it. If his office and authority are not to be compromised, no motion which fails to receive his approval should be carried, since a measure of apostolic authority remains in any episcopal church. Following the introduction of synodical government the relationship between the bishops and the General Synod has become unclear, with many consequential dangers for doctrine, and in years to come we may see a conflict between them despite the newly-received power of the General Synod to nominate new bishops to the Sovereign through the Prime Minister. Such placemen, however, will not always prove to be better Synod men than bishops.

The Roman Catholic Church, with which a great many Anglicans hope that one day their Church of England will be united, wisely declines to walk such a dubious synodical path, and the Church of England's adoption of synodical government may eventually prove to be an unsurmountable obstacle to such unity. Perhaps an ultimate desire for the re-establishment of authority in daily life generally may one day rectify the position which we have wantonly sacrificed in the Church of England in recent years, and it may be shown that a priest has greater authority in pastoral matters than a layman. For the moment, however, it is the day of the layman, even in decisions concerning the doctrine in which he is untrained, and it is not surprising that in the decade since the introduction of synodical government the strength and influence of the Church of England have plummeted to unbelievable depths. What the General Synod has done has generally been in defiance of rank-and-file opinion, as evidenced, for instance, by the poll conducted a few years ago in *Home Words*, the parish magazine inset which has the country's largest circulation (approaching a quarter of a million copies a month), which showed that at a time when twenty-seven diocesan synods were happily voting in favour of Disestablishment of the Church 95 per cent of churchgoers were against it.

The C of E is not a denomination, for presumably it is still the Church of the Nation, to which in theory at least and certainly by baptism all who do not choose to dissent from it belong. In recent years, however, the Church of England has slowly come to see itself in congregational terms, with parishioners in their tens of thousands forgotten or ignored in spite of their technical membership through their baptism long ago. Today, the great claims which the Church of England used to be proud to make – such as that of comprehensiveness – are quite forgotten as the General Synod pursues its tendentious way. The bearing which all this has had on the Church's teaching is obvious, and in consequence attendances now are only a pathetic fraction of what they were a century ago, the Church's sense of mission at home having become an early casualty. The Book of Common Prayer had to go because it had become a tombstone which reminded of the State connection and of former principles that had been betrayed. Morning and Evening Prayer, which could always be seen as mission services to which enquirers could come in order to get the flavour of Christianity, are now largely abandoned or seriously suffering, their place having been taken by the single morning service known as the Parish Communion (perhaps a hundred persons weekly in a parish of maybe twenty thousand or more), which to an enquirer must appear as an occasion for 'club' membership only. A South London church notice-board which recently proclaimed: 'The fellowship of Christ in this parish meets here every Sunday morning at 9.30 for the Parish Communion, with breakfast afterwards at the Vicarage' could be taken as implying that the maximum turnout of that alleged fellowship could never exceed a dozen. The supreme reproach of the present-day Church of England must be its apparent contentment with ministering to only a tiny fraction of those whom it should be representing, which is the inevitable result of having long ago ceased to value the Ministry of the Word in which not only the Scripture but the doctrine is expounded. Where the teaching fails, all fails.

The Church of England (Worship and Doctrine) Measure 1974 contains further important references to doctrine in Sections 4 (Safeguarding of doctrine) and 5 (Interpretation). Section 4 states:

> 4 (1) Every Canon or regulation making any such provision as is mentioned in section 1(1) of this Measure, every form of service or amendment thereof approved by the General Synod under any such Canon and every Canon making any such provision as is mentioned in section 2(1) of this Measure shall be such as in the opinion of the General Synod is neither contrary to, nor indicative of any departure from, the doctrine of the Church of England in any essential matter.
>
> (2) The final approval by the General Synod of any such Canon or regulation or form of service or amendment thereof shall conclusively determine that the Synod is of such opinion as aforesaid with respect to the matter so approved.

Section 5 states:

> 5 (1) References in this Measure to the doctrine of the Church of England shall be construed in accordance with the statement concerning that doctrine contained in the Canons of the Church

of England, which statement is in the following terms: 'The
doctrine of the Church of England is grounded in the holy
Scriptures, and in such teachings of the ancient Fathers and
Councils of the Church as are agreeable to the said Scriptures.
In particular such doctrine is to be found in the Thirty-Nine
Articles of Religion, the Book of Common Prayer, and the
Ordinal.'

Legislation which refers to opinion and requires action in accordance
with it is weak and can be dangerous. The requirement that such
opinion shall conform to the statement given in 5 (1) is unconvinc-
ing, especially in respect of the first-named repository of doctrine,
the Thirty-Nine Articles, the interpretation of which has long been
a matter of dispute. It is only right that such freedom of interpretation should be continued, but the combined effect of Sections 4(1)
and 5 would appear on the surface to fossilise doctrinal belief in the
Church of England as at the year 1562. However, as that is too
ridiculous to contemplate, it is possible that the real intention is a
tongue-in-cheek approval of a doctrinal future in which 'anything
goes' so long as in the opinion of the General Synod (if not in fact)
it accords with the listed formularies. It is all clever sophistry but
it has nothing to do with Christ, and there can surely be little
furtherance of the Gospel by a Measure whose 'Nay' is 'Yea'.
Although such a judgment may surprise some onlookers who hitherto have not paid much attention to what has been happening, it
will not surprise those who have examined closely the new services
which are already in wide use.

One of the more remarkable doctrinal changes involved in the
liturgical revision that has taken place is its depreciation of the sense
of sin. The General Confession at Morning and Evening Prayer of
1662 speaks of erring and straying from God's way and following
the devices of our own hearts, while under its guidance we say
'there is no health in us' and that 'we are miserable offenders' who
'have left undone those things which we ought to have done'. The
Communion of 1662 encourages us to take an even more serious
view of our situation, for we express ourselves there in these words:

Almighty God, Father of our Lord Jesus Christ, Maker of all
things, Judge of all men; We acknowledge and bewail our manifold sins and wickedness, Which we, from time to time, have
committed, By thought, word and deed, Against thy Divine Majesty, Provoking most justly thy wrath and indignation against us.
We do earnestly repent, And are heartily sorry for these our
misdoings; The remembrance of them is grievous unto us; the

burden of them is intolerable. Have mercy upon us, Have mercy upon us, most merciful Father . . .

If we have a sense of sin, and have sinned, it is right that we should confess properly and completely, and be men about it, if the real purpose is to clear the conscience and claim absolution. The revisers of the liturgy obviously felt that the terms used in that Confession are too abject in character for use today, for in its counterpart in Series 3 there is no reference to God as judge, to wickedness, God's wrath and indignation or the burden of misdoings, and the tone is comparatively casual and unemotional, with mention of 'ignorance', 'weakness' and 'fault', none of which is seen as 'intolerable'. The omission of the latter word is perhaps the principal pointer to the dogmatic change that has taken place. There is a feeling with the new version that, while there has to be a perfunctory 'going through the motions', it would really have been better if no Confession at all had been included. The changes that have been made represent beyond question a much reduced sense of sin, and therefore also of a need of penitence. Whereas an English congregation used to be a gathering of persons who saw themselves as sinners, their modern counterparts see themselves as comparatively sinless, thanks to the General Synod, whose opinion under Sections 4 and 5 of the Worship and Doctrine Measure doubtless is (as legally it must be) that this is 'neither contrary to, nor indicative of any departure from', the doctrine of the Church of England!

Is the sense of sin to come and go officially like this, subject to the fashion of the time? If we amend the Confession we are in fact amending the New Testament, in which there is a clear recognition that the roots of sin lie in a man's character. St Paul asserts its universality, St James says it begins in the human will and each man is responsible for his own wrongdoing, and the Johannine writings tell us it consists in disbelief in Christ and the consequent judgment. The New Testament, of course, tells us supremely that while sin had its most dire consequence in the death of Christ on the Cross, there, too, is the great antidote to it, for 'He is the propitiation for our sins', as St John said.

Formally, the dogma that Christ died for us and redeemed us by his blood is known as the Atonement, and it is the third of the three fundamental beliefs of the Christian religion, the other two being the Trinity and the Incarnation (that is, that God the Son took human nature). The Consecration Prayer in the 1662 Communion service expressed the Atonement simply and succinctly in undying words which may never be bettered, namely that Christ 'made, by

His one oblation of Himself once offered, a full, perfect, and sufficient sacrifice, oblation and satisfaction, for the sins of the whole
world', but this is not found in the Series 3 Communion. There, in
what is now called 'The Thanksgiving', we find 'Through him you
have freed us from the slavery of sin, giving him to be born as man,
to die upon the cross', and 'we celebrate and proclaim his perfect
sacrifice made once for all upon the cross', but these token references
to the Atonement are tame by comparison, and more selfish in
concept. In the Nicene Creed now it is not 'I believe' but 'We
believe' (which some see as appropriate for an apostate age), by
which change the sense of personal conviction of Christ's atoning
death is reduced. Will the General Synod go on to alter this to 'They
believe' (or possibly even to 'They believed') in due course? The
Atonement is a mystery which the Church does not define, though
there have been several theories. There is no doubt whatever that
not only Scripture but also two millennia of Christian experience
teach what the hymn 'There is a green hill' expresses so simply and
so well:

> He died that we might be forgiven,
> He died to make us good,
> That we might go at last to heaven,
> Saved by His precious blood.

Those who compiled the Book of Common Prayer had no doubt
about the sinfulness of the world in which they lived, and they led
the nation in appropriate contrition, ensuring that no one dared to
be complacent or to see himself as superior to that situation. The
General Synod, however, backing the liturgical revisers of today
and their Victorian view of inevitable progress supported by the
'come of age' philosophy, is of opinion that modern man inhabits
a much less sinful world that his forefathers; but how can they fly
in the face of human experience? The Revd Harold Goodwin has
written:

Look through any of today's newspapers; or sit back and think
quietly for a few minutes of the vast variety of sins that are
perpetrated every day in every section of society, from the parish
to the nation, from the nation to the whole world. Think, for
instance, of the dreadful statistics of road deaths, illegitimacy,
children in care, abortion, venereal disease, alcoholism, and criminal offences of all kinds here in Britain today. Or think of the
nations armed to the teeth against one another; and of the two
greatest nations, so afraid of each other that each has accumulated

weapons capable of destroying the whole human race in a matter almost of minutes, and manifestly prepared to unleash such powers of universal destruction if the tension between them should reach a degree that is by no means unthinkable. What can we say except that 'there is no health in us'? What can we plead less contrite than that 'we bewail our manifold sins and wickedness'; that 'we earnestly repent'; and that 'the burden' of our sinfulness 'is intolerable'?

The General Synod, though it is sworn not to make any provision which in its opinion indicates any departure from the doctrine of the Church of England, has nevertheless fallen for the idea that the horrors listed above are not of man's making but are the fault of 'them' rather than of 'us'. Strictly, in view of the state of man's world, our contrition now should be more abject than ever, not less; but such an outcome would not accord with the prevailing political climate, which has actually spawned many of the sins listed above and therefore must not be made to accept responsibility for them.

The decline and fall of the Book of Common Prayer since the celebration of its tercentenary in 1962 has been politically engineered, and the fact should be frankly stated. Those responsible could not forget the old adage that the Church of England was 'the Conservative Party at prayer', though that had slowly become less true with the passing of the years since the First World War. Writing in 1947 about the situation at the turn of the century Archbishop Garbett said: 'The Church . . . was strongly Conservative as opposed to the Liberalism of the Nonconformists . . . As a rule the Conservatives could still rely on the Church vote being cast in their favour.' Going on to describe the changes that could be observed fifty years later he said that the faith of the common man had come to be placed in political ideals, social rights or economic claims, for which he was often ready to fight and die, while faith in God made no appeal. In an analysis which is masterly in its detail (*The Claims of the Church of England*) the Archbishop could have gone on to say that the Conservative view remained the backbone of the Church, for obvious reasons. There is no doubt that until, say, the early sixties it was that unquestionably, for it alone showed respect for the past, which ecclesiastically centred chiefly on the Book of Common Prayer. Thus it came about that so far as the Socialist militants in the Church were concerned the Prayer Book had to go, willy-nilly and irrespective of any doctrine it enshrined, political considerations being seen as more important than any spiritual teaching – 'Back to your canvassing' one diocesan bishop is reputed to have said as he dismissed his clergy after a meeting. Socialist governments from 1964–70 and from 1974–9 ensured that episcopal appointments accelerated the take-over, though the Conservative government from 1970–74 did its best to apply a contrary process. That species of patronage is now ended, but another has arisen which might prove to maintain for a long while to come the Socialist dominance.

Whenever the Church makes a mistake it usually corrects it in the end by making the opposite mistake. While it is plainly wrong that the Conservatives should have dominated, as they undoubtedly did historically, in the life of the Church, it must also be wrong for the Socialists to do so now, for we must presume that the rank-and-file membership today reflects the fairly even Right and Left of the electorate. So long as the task of the Church is seen in political terms we shall ever be cursed with the desire for political domination and un-Christlike lust for power over others. If the Church must be seen as a democracy, then let it behave like one and grant rights to all, including something more than the euphemistic provision: 'the forms of service contained in the Book of Common Prayer continue to be available for use in the Church of England', which in fact is not being observed, for various reasons, although it is a proper democratic arrangement within the law of the land and the Church. It is a pity that the section in the Measure which deals with interpretation did not define the meaning of 'available', for in many churches the Book of Common Prayer is not available, in Sunday use or at any other time. It was wishful thinking on the part of those who drafted the Measure if they presumed that a sufficient quantity of Prayer Books for use by a fair-sized congregation would be kept readily available in parish churches which had opted for the alternative services; yet that is what the law would appear to require. 'Available for use' must mean at least thirty or forty copies, if the law is being taken seriously, rather than a single copy in the vestry or at the vicarage. Perhaps archdeacons, who are responsible for seeing the legalities are observed, might feel they should in their visitations enquire about the availability for use of the Book of Common Prayer in the parishes. It is to be hoped that the Prayer Book Society will maintain ceaseless vigilance in respect of availability, even to the point of checking on continuing production by the printers, especially following the publication of the 1980 prayer book. Perhaps it was with this sort of ecclesiastical situation in mind that Jesus advised his apostles to be 'wise as serpents' in Matt. 10:16. Thousands in the C of E have been 'unchurched' by petty popes in the parishes who have seen to it that only the alternative services are used, for political reasons; if an up-to-the-minute reason for an abysmal decline in the local influence of any parish church is sought, it could well be discovered there. We must accept with goodwill the use of the alternative services where they have been introduced with charity and commonsense, but at the same time it should be conceded that those who find such services unacceptable also have their rights and that they are far too many to be treated as expendable. The Standing Committee's advice to the General Synod (GS 107, 27 October 1972) stated: 'The 1662 Prayer Book and the services contained in it would remain available *to any congregation that desires to use them*' (my italics). We should remember that important piece of evidence.

. . . Common experience sheweth, that where a change hath been made of things advisedly established (no evident necessity so requiring) sundry inconveniences have thereupon ensued; and those many times more and greater than the evils, that were intended to be remedied by such change.

The Preface
Book of Common Prayer (1662)

Shakespeare and the Prayer Book
A. L. ROWSE

People who were brought up from childhood to go to church and attend services according to the Prayer Book in full flourish are more sharply (even nostalgically) attuned to the echoes of its phrases all through Shakespeare. There must be hundreds of such echoes, when one considers not only the liturgy but the lessons from the Bible that were read in church and the homilies that, in Elizabethan days, more often took the place of sermons – they were in fact sermons, for most of the clergy could not preach. There is hardly a play that does not somewhere or other echo something from the Psalms, and always from the Prayer Book version said or sung in church.

The influence of all this in shaping Shakespeare's mind and character should be clear enough, for its extent as reflected in his work is quite exceptional. The excellent old Stratford scholar, Edgar Fripp, estimated that 'his familiarity with the Bible is at least five times that of George Peele or Christopher Marlowe [in spite of their university education, we may add], or any contemporary dramatist.[1] It has been observed that up to about 1596–7 phrases from the Bishops' Bible predominate, and that was what was commonly used in church. After that phrases from the Genevan version are more numerous. It is thought that Shakespeare read in this popular text, a fairly cheap and convenient volume to possess – but again the phrases from the Psalms are always from the Prayer Book version he carried in his head.

He had an astonishing aural memory. Most educated Elizabethans must have had better memories than we have, for the whole of their education was based on memorising and memory-training. What is especially characteristic of him is the way that words catch in his ear, the concatenation of two words. In *Love's Labour's Lost* Rosaline (Berowne's i.e., Shakespeare's, Dark Lady) describes the young men of the Court: 'Well-liking wits they have: gross, gross: fat, fat.' Shakespeare's ear is echoing Psalm 92: 'They shall also bring forth more fruit in their age: and shall be fat and well-liking.' When Macbeth thinks of betraying Duncan like a Judas and killing him, he says: 'If it were done when 'tis done, then 'twere well it were done quickly . . .' Shakespeare's mind instinctively turns to Jesus's words, 'That thou doest, do quickly.'

Sometimes the concatenation is not immediate and the reference is more obscure. *Love's Labour's Lost* is full of jokes and puns, some of them now lost to us, for the play was a private skit on the Southampton circle by its poet – some of the characters recognisable in the play: e.g., the poet himself as Berowne, his dark mistress as Rosaline, Armado unmistakably Antonio Perez. A whole passage between Armado and Moth plays on the word green as the colour of lovers. When Armado says that Samson 'surely affected her for her wit', Moth retorts: 'It was so, sir, for she had a green wit.' The pun here is obscure to us, for we have not heard the Bishops' Bible phrasing: 'Samson answered her, "If they bind me with seven green withs [pronounced 'wits'] that were never dried, I shall be weak and be as another man." And the Philistines brought her seven withs that were yet green and were never dried, and she bound him therewith.' The reference back has been disputed on the ground that 'green wit' was a commonplace; well, it was – but the phrase occurs in the reiterated context of Samson, four times emphasised; and this makes the interpretation certain.

Another wit combat that may also be obscure to us today would not have been so to the Elizabethans, who had by law to go to church. In *The Comedy of Errors* we find:

Antipholus: Why, but there's many a man hath more hair than wit.
Dromio: Not a man of those but he hath the wit to lose his hair.
Antipholus: Why, thou didst conclude hairy men plain dealers without wit.
Dromio: The plainer dealer, the soonest lost; yet he loseth it in a kind of jollity.

The whole passage goes further with its bawdy suggestiveness which I need not elucidate; my point here is that it goes back to Holy Writ and is most revealing of our theme. For it refers to Jacob and Esau; the Geneva Bible tells us that Jacob was 'a plain man', and Esau 'rough', for which the Bishops' Bible has the word 'hairy'. Words and phrases stuck in Shakespeare's mind more tenaciously even than with most poets; for, towards the end of his working life, the concatenation comes up again in *The Winter's Tale*:

Clown: We are but plain fellows, sir.
Autolycus: A lie: you are rough and hairy.

It is fascinating to observe this combination of the Bishops' with the Geneva Bible, and reappearing over such a long span.

Phrases from the services of the church picked up from the Prayer Book echo and re-echo through all the plays. Chiefly from Matins and Evensong, of course, for those were the principal services to the Elizabethans. Communion service was much less frequent, though communicating at Easter was obligatory. From the Catechism comes Hamlet's description of his hands as 'these pickers and stealers': one answers in the Catechism that it is one's duty 'to keep my hands from picking and stealing.' (I well remember the impression the phrase made on me as a child.) From the Catechism too comes the phrase 'special grace'.[2] When Shakespeare cites the Commandments, he does so in the Prayer Book form: 'Thou shalt do no murder'; or 'visit the sins of the fathers upon the children unto the third and fourth generation of them that hate me' – this recurs in:

> Thy sins are visited in this poor child. . .
> Being but the second generation.
> *King John*, II. i. 179–81

The phrase 'amend your lives' is repeated several times in the liturgy, at Morning and Evening Prayer, in the Communion service and the Litany: one was hardly allowed to forget it. 'Confess yourselves to Almighty God, with full purpose of amendment of life.' Prince Henry says to Falstaff: 'I see a good amendment of life in thee'; Falstaff carries on to Bardolph, 'Do thou amend thy face, and I'll amend my life.' It is the juxtaposition of the two words that is so telling, and so characteristic of Shakespeare: 'amend' or 'amendment', together with 'life'. When the Prince jokes about the old reprobate's amendment of life, he has the answer. 'Why, Hal, 'tis my vocation, Hal; 'tis no sin for a man to labour in his vocation.' What a joke when one thinks what Falstaff's vocation was! For the whole Prayer Book enjoins that we should labour in our vocation. The Catechism teaches that it is one's duty 'to labour truly to get mine own living'; the Homily or Sermon against Idleness bids everyone 'in some kind of labour to exercise himself, according as the vocation whereunto God hath called him shall require.' So too the Epistles, heard read during the Communion Service.

The Devil quotes Shakespeare for his own purpose, and one aspect of the multifarious Falstaff is as the Vice (or Devil) of the old morality plays. So he can preach, with reverberations from the Collects: 'Well, God give thee the spirit of persuasion, and him the ears of profiting, that what thou speakest may move, and what he hears may be believed.' The phrase from the Litany, 'O God, we have heard with our ears' – here is the conjunction of 'heard' with 'ears', which I found funny as a choirboy. So, too, did Sir Hugh Evans in *The Merry Wives of Windsor*: 'What phrase is this, "He hears with ear"? Why, it is affectatious.' I thought it merely repetitious.

Among the words we can never forget are those in the General Confession. 'We have left undone those things which we ought to have done.' This is reflected in 'their best conscience is not to leave't undone, but kept unknown.' (*Othello*, III.iii. 207–8)
Or again, 'Hear what comfortable words our Saviour Christ saith', is addressed to us by the priest in the Communion service. This reappears at a crisis in *Richard II*: 'For God's sake, speak comfortable words.' We can remember that the word 'comfort' had a much stronger meaning to the Elizabethans: it meant to strengthen. 'The Holy Ghost, the Comforter', meant the strengthener, who gave one strength.

Phrases like 'to weep with them that weep', to be 'in adversity', 'they know not what they do' may crop up anywhere in the plays – the last in different forms in several of them. In *The Comedy of Errors*, when Dromio of Syracuse is all mixed up, begins almost to doubt his own identity, he says, 'Nay, 'tis for me to be patient: I am in adversity.' It is the two words coming together that give one the clue – the audience would recognise from church service, 'that thou mayest give him patience in time of adversity.' It is this that would raise a laugh – and also shows us that the phrase has a point, is not a commonplace. 'Lord, have mercy upon us' became a commonplace, uttered on thousands of lips at any time, especially in time of trouble; it occurs again and again in the Liturgy, whence it no doubt sprang into use.

Sometimes, as with Dromio's 'patience in adversity', these echoes are turned to comic effect, as again with Falstaff or Mistress Quickly. We are amused to hear her claim that she is 'the weaker vessel', or Falstaff of all people sigh, 'Oh, if men were to be saved by merit! . . . ' For this not only goes back to St Paul and justification by faith, but more immediately to the Homily on Fasting – a nice authority for a Falstaff!

We may resume concisely, with Fripp, the phrases that Shakespeare re-echoed from service in church: absolution and remission; grafted inwardly in our hearts, in the imagination of their hearts, love, honour and obey; Good Lord, deliver us; grant us thy peace, world without end. These words and phrases came through more stirringly, more freshly, to the Elizabethans, for they were newly minted – largely by Archbishop Cranmer who, it is touching to think, might well have lived to crown Elizabeth I as he had baptised her, if only he had not been burned by Mary. We might make the point here that in all Shakespeare's work there is no trace of his acquaintance with the Roman missal or the Vulgate. There are, however, traces of his acquaintance with the Metrical Psalms that were sung in church.

The Anglican emphasis on charity, in the complex concept of love, presumably derives from the Vulgate's rendering *caritas*. This appears in the conclusion of Berowne–Shakespeare's argument in *Love's Labour Lost:*

> For charity itself fulfils the law,
> And who can sever love from charity?

In the next Act Rosaline addresses her Princess as

> My red dominical, my golden letter.

This refers to the letter to mark Sundays, the dominical day, in calendar or prayer book. And we notice Shakespeare's familiarity with the seasons and festivals, the customs and usages of the Church: 'earthly godfathers'[3] – his own twins, Hamnet and Judith, were called after Hamnet and Judith Sadler, Stratford neighbours, pretty certainly godparents, as he himself was to young William Walker, 'my godson', to whom he left 20s. in gold in his will. In his earlier plays he refers, as the Church did, to Pentecost; in later plays it becomes Whitsun. The feasts and the saints appear: 'his child is a year and a quarter old, come Philip and Jacob:'[4] i.e., the feast of St Philip and St James. And in an earlier play, like *Love's Labour's Lost*, Solomon and the Queen of Sheba appear in their earlier forms, Salomon and Saba, as in church.

As we have seen, the Homilies went along with the Prayer Book, for as the Preface of 1562 said, 'all they which are appointed ministers have not the gift of preaching sufficiently to instruct the people which is committed unto them.' The Puritans (whom Shakespeare, like all theatre-people, disliked) made a great point of sermonising. The Queen's answer was very much to the point: how many of the clergy were capable of preaching? Only some five hundred, out of nine thousand parishes. Moreover, she did not encourage their preaching – it led to disputes and contentiousness. The Book of Homilies, with its sound, considered doctrine, was to be preferred. (I am old enough to have heard it used, and a sermon read from it, in my own parish church.)

In *As You Like It* – which is in several respects close to Shakespeare's own background – there is a direct reference in Rosalind's 'O most gentle pulpiter, what tedious homily of love have you wearied your parishioners withal, and never cried "Have patience, good people"?' Several of the themes of these sermons recur in the plays and are given considerable development in them. That against Swearing and Perjury is reflected again and again. In it people were admonished against taking an unlawful oath, or performing it. In *2 Henry VI* we find:

> It is great sin to swear unto a sin,
> But greater sin to keep a sinful oath.

We find much more about oath-breaking in the early plays, and particularly again in regard to Henry of Navarre's going back on his Protestantism in order to win Paris and recommend himself to France as king.

Even greater extension is given in the plays to the themes of the homily of Obedience and that on Disobedience and Wilful Rebellion. When Shakespeare was a boy of five or six Stratford received the call to arms against the Northern rebels of 1569–70, and sent its quota of men and arms to the North. The Book ends with a prayer of thanksgiving for its suppression. The language of these sermons remained on in that retentive air.

> Almighty God hath created and appointed all things in heaven, earth and waters, in a most excellent and perfect order. In heaven he hath appointed distinct and several orders and states of arch-angels and angels. In earth he hath assigned and appointed kings, princes, with other governors under them, in all good and necessary order. The sun, moon, stars, rainbow, thunder, lightning, clouds, and all the birds of the air do keep their order.

In *Troilus and Cressida*, written with the fatal consequences of Essex' (and Southampton's) wilful disobedience and rebellion much in mind, this becomes:

> The heavens themselves, the planets and this centre,
> Observe degree, priority and place,
> Insisture, course, proportion, season, form,
> Office and custom, in all line of order.

When degree is undermined and order in society breaks down:

> Take away kings, rulers, princes, magistrates, judges and such estates of God's order, no man shall ride or go by the highway unrobbed, no man shall sleep in his own house or bed unkilled,

no man shall keep his wife, children and possession in quietness, all things shall be common, and there must needs follow all mischief and utter destruction both of souls, bodies, goods and commonwealth.

This is echoed in:

Take but degree away, untune that string,
And hark what discord follows. . .
Strength should be lord of imbecility,
And the rude son should strike his father dead.

The sermon brings home the consequences to the individual: 'the brother to seek and often to work the death of his brother, the son of his father.' In one of his earliest plays, *3 Henry VI*, the dramatist has the scene: 'Alarum. Enter a son that hath killed his father, at one door; and a father that hath killed his son, at another door.'

What general conclusions can we draw from all this, what indications does it give as to the man and his work? It is already indicated that he was neither a Puritan nor a Catholic, that he was an upholder of the social order of a conservative kind, not a restless, challenging spirit like Marlowe, nor a turbulent one like Ben Jonson. Tact was of the essence of his spirit, political and social tact – he would never give trouble to authority, and never did; personal tact too – everybody described him as 'gentle', which in Elizabethan English meant gentlemanly. He was a conformist, a family man who recognised his social and neighbourly obligations – his will shows that; again unlike Marlowe and Ben Jonson in their different ways.

We have seen that in his numerous and frequent echoes from the Bible, he moved from that used in church to the pocket Bible one could carry – for what that indicates, probably a matter of convenience. However, his Anglican usage was conservative – in that like the Queen's – to judge from his language: the frequent use of traditional terms like 'priest', or 'by the Mass', or references to holy water (no longer in use).

We may get a further, more specific indication by comparing the early plays with the later for the echoes we are listening to with him. In his first history play, *1 Henry VI*, I have counted over a dozen echoes of Prayer Book, Bible and Homilies. To take only a few: Henry VI appeals to his quarrelling lords to join 'in love and amity', the Prayer Book conjunction of words; 'in the mouth of every sucking babe' echoes the Metrical Version of Psalm 8. Bed-

ford, dying, says: 'Now, quiet soul, depart when heaven please, For
I have seen our enemies' overthrow.' This echoes the Nunc Dimittis
at Evening Prayer: 'Lord, now lettest thou thy servant depart in
peace. . . For mine eyes have seen thy salvation.' How unforgettable
the words and their rhythm are! What clinches the matter once
more is the conjunction of the two – 'depart' and 'have seen'. 'The
blood of innocents' again conjoins two words, 'the cry of innocent
blood' from Deuteronomy.

I have noticed some eight echoes from the Bible; and from the
Homilies we have these phrases, 'wilful disobedience, and rebellion',
and 'effusion of blood' which is the phrase in the sermons against
Disobedience and Wilful Rebellion. Notice the characteristic trans-
position, quite frequent in these phrases, conscious or unconscious,
probably for artistic variation.

The references back in the earliest tragedy, Senecan and Ovidian
as *Titus Andronicus* is, are naturally overwhelmingly classical. But
the Prayer Book is there, in 'she drinks no other drink but tears',
from 'plenteousness of tears to drink'. Marooned on my headland
in Cornwall without a Bishops' Bible conveniently by me, I cannot
say whether the Cain reference is to that – it does not greatly signify;
but of the line, 'A charitable wish and full of love,' we are told that
'of the main sixteenth-century versions, only the Bishops' Bible read
charity.'[5] Here again we have the Anglican association of love with
caritas, continuous with the Catholic tradition.

Fripp tells us that 'Cain gripped him from the first. He refers to
the story of this "primal" murderer not less than twenty-five times.
Others seized on him with only less tenacity.'[6] Among those that
recur most frequently are Job, some twenty-five times, Judas
twenty-one, John the Baptist (though not named) ten, Samson and
the Prodigal son nine each, Herod eight, Jephthah, Peter, Pilate,
Lazarus and even the Whore of Babylon seven each. 'Satan suggests
many. To the teaching of Paul, and to the ministry of Christ, the
references are multitudinous.'

The Prodigal Son comes into the early *Comedy of Errors*, where
we should not expect many religious references. But Dromio of
Syracuse suggests three in one short speech: 'Not that Adam that
kept the Paradise, but that Adam that keeps the prison: he that goes
in the calf's skin that was killed for the Prodigal; he that came
behind you, sir, like an evil angel, and bid you forsake your liberty.'
It was a good angel that liberated Peter from prison in the Acts of
the Apostles. We find this counterposing of angels several times
contemporaneously in the Sonnets, notably in the line, 'Till my bad

angel fire my good one out.' Both the early *Comedy of Errors* and *The Two Gentlemen of Verona* refer to Whitsun as Pentecost.

When we come to the two last plays, *The Tempest* and *Henry VIII*, there is a striking diminution of such references, echoes of such phrases, though the late plays are suffused with Christian virtues, charity, reconciliation, forgiveness, acceptance. He had always subscribed to a Christian view of the universe and man's place in it, his mind deeply engaged by moral issues emerging into orthodox ethical teaching, again a conforming spirit – not a heterodox challenging one like Marlowe. But echoes from Bible or Prayer Book hardly occur at all. What does it mean? That these echoes from earlier days were fainter now? That he went to church much less?

In Elizabethan days it was obligatory to attend church: if one did not, fines and ultimately imprisonment followed. When residing at home in Stratford, Shakespeare would go to church with the family or he would have been noticed and cited – as his father was, when his affairs went downhill, and he kept away to avoid process for debt being served on him. But when in London, where William was only a lodger – the family parked at Stratford – it would not be noticeable whether he went to church or no: he was not a parishioner. The whole family of his patron, both Southampton's and his mother's, were Catholics: that evidently did not constitute any problem. Tact, more even than ripeness, was all – and Southampton was not an aggressive Catholic like his father[7]: when James came to the throne and let him out of the Tower, he became a Protestant.

Everything shows that the family at Stratford were regular church-going Protestants, when some of their neighbours remained Catholic. All John and Mary Shakespeare's children were christened in church, and some of them buried – the youngest girl, Anne, for instance, with a special fee for 'the bell and pall' on 4 April 1579.[8] The youngest son, Edmund, was christened in church on 3 May 1580; he followed his successful eldest brother into the theatre, but died young, in the frozen winter of 1607, and was buried in St Saviour's, Southwark (now the Cathedral), on the last day of the year 'with a forenoon knell of the great bell.' We need hardly conjecture who paid for that.

Similarly with the weddings: Shakespeare's daughter married her doctor husband, John Hall, on 5 June 1607, Judith her Thomas Quiney in church on 10 February 1616, only a couple of months before her father's death. When he came to draw up his will, it began with the regular formula of a Protestant churchman: 'I commend my soul into the hands of God my Creator, hoping and assuredly believing through the only merits of Jesus Christ my Saviour to be made partaker of life everlasting.' He died, as he lived, a conforming member of the Church of England – rather like its tolerant undogmatic Supreme Governor, the Queen herself, whom he well knew, and after whom his only grandchild, last of his stock, was called.

There in the chancel of the parish church where he was christened his immediate family are gathered together: he and his wife, Anne, the clever daughter Susanna, who was his heir and her husband, and the grandchild Elizabeth's first husband, Thomas Nash. The pieces, like all the evidences, fall in place and conform.

References
1 Edgar I. Fripp, *Shakespeare, Man and Artist*, Oxford University Press, 1938, p 101.
2 *Love's Labour's Lost*, I.i.150.
3 I.i.88.
4 *Measure for Measure*, III.ii.190.
5 J. C. Maxwell's edition of *Titus Andronicus* (New Arden Shakespeare), p 83.
6 Fripp, p 98.
7 Cf. my *Shakespeare's Southampton, Patron of Virginia*, Macmillan, 1965, chapter 2.
8 Mark Eccles, *Shakespeare in Warwickshire*, University of Wisconsin Press, 1961, p 27.

Compare the vitality of language implicit in
Shakespeare, in the Book of Common Prayer or in the
style of a country gentleman such as Cavendish, with
our present vulgate. 'Motivation researchers', those
grave-diggers of literate speech, tell us that the perfect
advertisement should neither contain words of more
than two syllables nor sentences with dependent
clauses. In the United States, millions of copies have
been printed of 'Shakespeare' and the 'Bible' in the
form of comic-strips with captions in basic English.

GEORGE STEINER
Language and Silence

Liturgy and literature
BRIAN MORRIS

In an advertisement in a London tube train, Ratners the Jewellers showed pictures of the loving couple gazing together at their wedding ring (which the advertisers, naturally, suggested might be purchased from them on advantageous terms) and accompanied the pictures with the following words: 'With this ring I thee wed, with my body I thee worship, and with all my worldly goods I thee endow.' I find it more than moderately interesting that in 1979 the advertising industry should choose those words from the 1662 Book of Common Prayer rather than the up-to-date, 'modern English', contemporary, meaningful and relevant words which replace them in the Series 3 Marriage Service:

> I give you this ring
> as a sign of our marriage.
> With my body I honour you,
> all that I am I give to you,
> and all that I have I share with you.

Perhaps the advertisers felt that the new words were not yet sufficiently well known to be recognised by bemused travellers, perhaps the traditional words were simply felt to be more 'romantic', perhaps they obscurely felt that a phrase like 'all that I am I give to you' belonged more to the world of the BeeGees and the Stranglers than to the world of the Solemnization of Matrimony which they were trying to conjure up. The point is that a commercial firm of advertisers, acutely conscious of the persuasive powers of language and professionally sensitive to those verbal 'triggers' which make people buy things, coldly calculated that there was good mileage for their purposes in the words of Cranmer's liturgy.

In doing so, they accepted the risk of being imperfectly understood. The word 'worship' in a context like this one had shifted in meaning and connotation since 1662, and if the average bridegroom seriously believed that by repeating those words he was actually making a legal deed of gift to his bride of all his assets, including his motor bike, his bank balance and his collection of LPs, he might send the ring back to Ratners and request a refund of his expenditure. The advertisers obviously felt the risks were justified for the emotional effect the time-honoured phraseology might have on that hard-bitten cross-section of humanity that travels on the London Underground.

They realised, in short, that the language of the past has a power in the present – a perception which seems to have eluded both the Anglican and Roman Catholic revisers of our liturgies. The point about the past is that it will not go away; it follows at your heel like a well-trained spaniel; it dogs you. T. S. Eliot stated it memorably in 'Burnt Norton':

> Time past and time future
> What might have been and what has been
> Point to one end, which is always present.

The past, and the language of the past, is alive in the present whenever we evoke it, or use it, or think about it. In so far as a significant section of society chooses to use Cranmer's words or the words of the Authorised Version of the Bible those words are alive in the present and relevant to our contemporary concerns. They form an inalienable part of 'modern English'.

It is, of course, all a matter of degree. At one time, most members of the Society of Friends used to address each other and write to each other using the second person singular of the possessive pronoun – 'I have not seen thee since Friday, and thou still owest me five pounds' – but the practice has dwindled, and 'thee' and 'thou' are now confined to dialect usage, though that usage is remarkably widespread in Britain and pertinaciously persistent. The revisers of the Anglican liturgy decided some time ago that it was no longer necessary, or appropriate, to use those forms in addressing the first person of the Trinity in public worship. For all I know, there may be compelling theological reasons for calling God 'you', but the case cannot be argued on the grounds that 'thee' and 'thou' are not 'modern English'. You can hear them used quite unselfconsciously in a public bar in Barnsley or on the stage at Stratford-on-Avon. They pass quite unnoticed, they are perfectly comprehensible, and they have no smack of archaism or anachronism. But the revisers felt that these special forms of address to God ought to go. So that the forms of worship should be 'better understanded of the people' they are rewritten in the language we all understand, the language of our time: modern English.

There is no such thing as 'modern English', or if there is it is beyond the wit of scholars of language to define it or isolate it. The language currently in use in speech and writing by native speakers of our tongue is so complex and multifarious, so perpetually developing and shifting, that no one person or group can justly claim to comprehend it or command it. Examine a few examples, in written form but designed to be spoken aloud to different hearers:

1 I swear by Almighty God that the evidence I shall give shall be the truth, the whole truth, and nothing but the truth.

2 What I am saying is that we are not having any of the baked beans in stock currently, and I am not to be expecting them while Friday.

3 Well, her and me we went to this party, didn't we, y'know what I mean, and well there was this fella there wasn't there, and well need I say more, I mean, bleeding hell. . .

4 Our policies are the right policies, the best policies, the policies you've asked for, the commonsense policies, the policies that are going to make Britain Great again. . .

5 Football, and Harry Haslam's Sheffield United look set for the big drop into Division 3 unless club-record signing Alex Sabella from River Plate can turn on the magic tonight. . .

6 The implementation of this policy required a commitment to a greatly increased effort in mineral exploration, both in terms of expenditure and skilled human resources.

All these are pieces of living modern English: they might be heard (respectively) in court, in a Pakistani shop in Bradford, on a building site, on the hustings, on a local radio programme, and in a company board room. Examples could be endlessly multiplied, since modern English is spoken in the United States, Nigeria, Singapore and Sydney, and in describably different ways. Anyone who undertakes the hazardous task of modernising a traditional text must be aware of the vast range of possibilities and the delicate discriminations which determine the intuitively recognised boundaries between one linguistic group and another within the same language. Above all, he must recognise the 'register' of the language which is appropriate to his work. This question of 'register' is one which increasingly interests students and scholars of the science of language. It probably derives from the organist's practice of creating various patterns of sound and tone-colour on his instrument by the use of different combinations of stops. Each combination creates a 'register', and the quality of an organist's performance of a piece is to some extent evaluated by considering the aptness of the registration he has selected. The analogy holds good in the evaluation of literary performance, and provides the literary critic with a useful tool for analysis and judgment. Obviously, example 6 above makes use of that register of English which is appropriate to the formal, public description of a 'policy' matter in the fields of industry, or commerce, or government, and it presupposes that its hearers will be acquainted with the vocabulary involved and find the 'tone of voice' acceptable. It could easily be rewritten in a simplified form: 'To do this, we had to find new mines, and put money and miners into them.' But that way of putting it would be out of key with the normal, accepted verbal procedures in the conduct of company business. Example 6 could certainly not be rewritten in the style of example 3 without providing both a stumbling-block and foolishness.

Liturgy is normally considered to belong to that register of the language which is reserved for the expression of man's deepest thoughts and feelings, which uses rich, powerful and often technical, abstract vocabulary, and strongly rhythmical, sometimes repetitive, phraseology. Its imagery is often a form of symbolism or shorthand, comprehensible to the initiated but without much more than surface meaning to the outsider. To speak of 'the Lamb of God', for example, suggests easily and immediately to a Christian congregation the second person of the Trinity, the sacrificial oblation of Christ, the innocence of Him that was without sin, and the historical continuity of the Judaeo-Christian tradition. To an outsider – say, a Yoruba priest of the cult of Ogun in West Africa – it does not, of itself, suggest any of these things. The potency of an image depends on the presuppositions of its audience. Whoever it was, in the distant past, who first described Jesus as 'God's lamb' created a brilliant metaphor, bringing together several hitherto unrelated aspects of Jesus's significance. The effect on the original audience must have been startling and enlightening and memorable. But, like everything else, metaphors decay in time, and the richest metaphors degenerate into the deepest clichés:

> In those halcyon days a King ruled fancy-free. He could sort the wheat from the chaff without shedding any crocodile tears. But nowadays, it's a different kettle of fish, a horse of a different colour. . .

Who, reading that, sees in his mind's eye the cobalt blue of the kingfisher, the phantasm, the spectre, the ghost which lurks behind the word 'fancy'? Who understands threshing, or would recognise a flail if he fell over one? What is the difference between two kettles of fish, and why 'kettles', anyway? The living roots of these dead images are superbly explored in Archbishop R. C. Trench's book

On the Study of Words, which should be compulsory reading in every theological college. But it was first published in 1851 and it is hard to come by nowadays. Trench, explaining a word like 'sacrament' lays bare its etymology and displays the imagery behind the word. Such a word is a most tuneful 'stop' in the religious register of our language, but it has been banished completely from the Anglican Series 3 services by the revisers of our liturgy. Since there can be no compelling theological reasons for the abandonment of the concept, one can only assume that the word was not felt to be 'modern English'.

To some extent, the liturgical revisers are swimming with the tide. The 'religious register' of English is not a powerful and evident presence in contemporary speech and writing. One can recognise it easily in the literature of the past, even the quite recent past. Wordsworth, writing of

A presence that disturbs me with the joy
Of elevated thoughts; a sense sublime
Of something far more deeply interfused,
Whose dwelling is the light of setting suns,
And the round ocean and the living air,
And the blue sky, and in the mind of man. . .

sounds the note quite clearly. One can point to it everywhere in Blake. His imagery, vocabulary, rhythms, tone, and above all the quality of elevated seriousness with which he summons up the creatures of his imagination, are redolent of their origins in Hebraic poetry and the English prose of the Authorised Version:

The sea fowl takes the wintry blast for a cov'ring to her limbs,
And the wild snake the pestilence to adorn him with gems and
    gold;
And trees & birds & beasts & men behold their eternal joy.
Arise, you little glancing wings, and sing your infant joy!
Arise, and drink your bliss, for everything that lives is holy!

The use of the religious register is apparent in some of the poems of Emily Brontë, though at a greater remove from specifically Christian vocabulary:

Then dawns the Invisible, the Unseen its truth reveals;
My outward sense is gone, my inward essence feels –
Its wings are almost free, its home, its harbour found;
Measuring the gulf it stoops, and dares the final bound!

The response such a passage elicits from the reader comes not from specific reference, but from the way a word like 'dawns' is in touch with 'reveals' in the same line, and from the way 'wings' hints at the angelic while still remaining a firm image of a butterfly emerging from its chrysalis. 'Harbour,' too, has its connotations of the end of life's voyage, and the final line summons up a light reminiscence of the theologian's traditional image of 'the leap of faith'. Emily Brontë's poem manifestly faces the same order of mystery as the lines quoted above from Wordsworth's *Tintern Abbey*, and both make delicate use of techniques of allusion and the associations of words to link their utterance with the great body of overtly religious literature.

But writing in the religious register need not be confined to the expression of religious or speculative concepts. Nor is it confined to poetry. The following passage was written by a novelist who firmly rejected the tenets of organised religion; it is objective and detached rather than personal, but the provenance of its style is unquestionably biblical:

> Nature repairs her ravages – but not all. The uptorn trees are not rooted again; the parted hills are left scarred: if there is a new growth, the trees are not the same as the old, and the hills underneath their green vesture bear the marks of the past rending. To the eyes that have dwelt on the past, there is no thorough repair.

That is George Eliot, in the final chapter of *The Mill on the Floss*. The thought would be familiar and acceptable to the writers of the books of Job or Ecclesiastes, and the balanced parallelism in the phraseology derives from the poetic structures of the Psalmist.

The balanced, answering, antithetical structures of the Psalms are obviously a formative influence on the prose style of D. H. Lawrence, and in passages where he is describing moods of raised passion – be they of love or revulsion – he habitually relies on an evocation of Hebrew poetry, combining it with a use of vocabulary which shows the inversions, doublets and repetitions so characteristic of liturgical writing. This passage, from *The Rainbow*, is typical of a thousand:

> All the blood in his body went black and powerful and corrosive as he heard her. Black and blind with hatred of her he was. He was in a very black hell, and could not escape.
>
> He hated her for what she said. Did he not give her everything, was she not everything to him? And the shame was a bitter fire in that she was everything to him, that he had nothing but her.

And then that she should taunt him with it, that he could not escape!

To the making of prose like that many influences have contributed. But strongly present among the ingredients are rhythmic constructions like the opening of Psalm 54:

Save me, O God, for thy Name's sake: and avenge me in thy strength.
Hear my prayer, O God: and hearken unto the words of my mouth.

Lawrence's structure of variation and repetition is strikingly like what we find at heightened moments in liturgy; for example, in the Gloria:

O Lord God, Lamb of God, Son of the Father, that takest away the sins of the world, have mercy upon us. Thou that takest away the sins of the world, have mercy upon us. Thou that takest away the sins of the world, receive our prayer. . . .

As F. R. Leavis has pointed out, Lawrence is a major author in the great tradition of the English novel, and part of his achievement lies in his instinctive ability to operate commandingly and convincingly in the religious register of English at moments of special passion or perception.

It is a melancholy fact that no novelist since Lawrence has displayed anything approaching the same command. Indeed, the shift in the styles available to the novelist has been towards the other end of the spectrum. Perhaps the most influential style in the second half of the twentieth century has been that of Samuel Beckett. The opening of his novel *Murphy* indicates the present predilection for all that is flat, unassertive and unevocative in recent prose:

The sun shone, having no alternative, on the nothing new. Murphy sat out of it, as though he were free, in a mew in West Brompton. Here for what might have been six months he had eaten, drunk, slept, and put his clothes on and off, in a medium-sized cage of north-western aspect commanding an unbroken view of medium-sized cages of south-eastern aspect. Soon he would have to make other arrangements, for the mew had been condemned.

This, and it is typical of so much of Beckett, is deliberately anti-rhetorical, rejecting all that is colourful, incantatory, dramatic, in favour of apparent prosaic translucence, and endless gradation of irony. It is an expressive and subtle medium for Beckett's nihilistic vision of the universe and man's paltry place in it, a vision which manages to be at once boring, intriguing, and richly comic. Nothing could be further from the intensities and perfervidness of Lawrence. Nothing could be more completely alienated from the religious register of the language. Yet Beckett's dry, ironic, reductive and undeceived voice is very much a voice of our times; indeed, some would maintain that he is the perfect spokesman for contemporary humanity in the age of anxiety.

There is no easily available religious language even for poets who are specifically concerned with religious experience. Geoffrey Hill, one of the most sensitive and accomplished poets now writing, and one deeply concerned with the religious dimension of human life though he would not describe himself as an orthodox Christian, uses the whole corpus of traditional religious images, symbols, rhythms and locutions in his attempts to extend the boundaries of spiritual awareness. He does so consciously, and in the belief that there are no adequate substitutes in the language for these forms. His most recent volume, *Tenebrae* (1978), begins with a poem in fifteen short, self-contained sections, 'The Pentecost Castle'; section four illustrates Hill's religious language and the use to which he puts it:

> At dawn the Mass
> burgeons from stone
> A Jesse tree
> of resurrection
>
> budding with candle
> flames with gold
> and white wafers
> of the feast
>
> and ghosts for love
> void a few tears
> of wax upon
> forlorn altars

Apart from the terse, sparse economy of the lines themselves there are a few factual keys here, without which meaning could not be unlocked. Unless one knows that a Jesse tree is a family tree (usually found in a church window, as at Wells Cathedral, St George's, Hanover Square, or Dorchester Abbey, near Oxford) tracing the descent of Jesus from the royal line of David, with the intermediary descendants placed on scrolls of foliage branching out of each other, it would not be possible to appreciate the delicate set of correspondences being set up in the first stanza between the dawn and the resurrection, the sacrifice of the Mass and the tree which is the family tree, the tree of life, the 'tree' of Calvary, and the tree in nature which comes to life at the dawn of every year. The point is that Geoffrey's Hill's use of religious language takes him deeply back into the iconographic and liturgical traditions of Christianity. And a successful reader of his poems must know, or be prepared to learn, his language. It is not surprising that very few people understand what he is talking about. He is a difficult poet who makes no concessions to the under-educated. He may write about the Mass, but it is not for the masses. Geoffrey Hill's poetry illustrates the way a very distinguished writer feels he must go in the use of religious language. Instead of bringing the sacred images up to date, and making the mysteries of the faith intelligible to the secularised audience, he burrows back into the rich deposits of the past. He uses the great traditional images confidently, without explanation, and makes unashamedly severe demands on his readers. His way of extending the boundaries of spiritual understanding involves bringing the past into the present with all its accumulated luggage.

The liturgical revisers of recent years have followed precisely the opposite path. In an attempt to make liturgy meaningful to those who are ecclesiastically sub-normal in educational attainment they have largely jettisoned the poetic richnesses of traditional images, and attempted to 'make it new'. One tiny example of this is provided by the version of the Nicene Creed which occurs in the Anglican Series 3 Order for Holy Communion. The pre-Reformation Latin included the phrase '*Et incarnatus est de Spiritu Sancto ex Maria Virgine: Et homo factus est*'. Since 1549 this has been rendered in English as 'And was incarnate by the Holy Ghost of the Virgin Mary, And was made man'. The Church, in its teaching, made a meaningful distinction between the Incarnation and the Nativity. The doctrine of the Incarnation affirmed that the eternal Son of God was translated from the realm of spirit and took human flesh from his human mother, so that the historical Christ is at once fully God and fully man. The Nativity was the actual historical event of the birth of Jesus. The one is a theological doctrine, the other an event which occurred at a particular time in a particular place. Series 3 obliterates this distinction:

> by the power of the Holy Spirit
> he was born of the Virgin Mary,
> and became man.

Phraseology such as this appears to simplify things and make them clear, but in fact it does not. What is this 'power' of the Holy Spirit? In what way did it cause Jesus to be born? The Latin offers a delicate sexual metaphor, following the tradition of the Gospels. The grammatical positioning of '*de*' and '*ex*' suggests a male and female participation. '*By* the Holy Ghost *of* the Virgin Mary' is, in its precise way, not unlike the way we still (in modern English) describe the breeding of a racehorse, *by* Red Rum *out of* Saucy Sue. The sexual metaphor is, of course, as crude and inadequate to describe the mystery of the Incarnation as the garden image is to describe the pre-lapsarian Paradise or the tree and the apple to account for the Fall of Man. But it offers a point of entry; it allows the mind a freedom to speculate and imagine. The Series 3 alternative positively prohibits thought, since the 'power of the Holy Spirit' is such an abstraction that it can make no metaphoric contact with the concrete picture summoned up by 'he was born'. The modern worshipper, faced with the revised Nicene Creed, is cut off from his due inheritance.

The iconoclastic attitude of the revisers towards imagery is only part of a larger strategy. From the very best of motives, no doubt, the official bodies charged with the terrible task of liturgical revision within the Anglican Communion (and the same tendency can be observed among Roman Catholics as well) have undertaken a campaign of all-out simplification. 'Nothing said not understood' might have been the motto emblazoned on the wall, and 'Sing ye praises with understanding' could have been their campaign anthem – were it not for the 'ye'! This is nowhere more evident than in the revised attitude towards Sin. The 1662 version of The Book of Common Prayer took Sin very seriously; we had our noses rubbed in it regularly and we were constantly exhorted to amendment of life. The Order for Morning Prayer, for example, began with an invitation 'to acknowledge and confess our manifold sins and wickedness; and that we should not dissemble nor cloke them before the face of Almighty God our heavenly Father; but confess them with an humble, lowly, penitent, and obedient heart; to the end that we may obtain forgiveness of the same by his infinite goodness and mercy.' All this is swept away in Series 3, and replaced by a lightly modernised version of 1 John 1:8–9.

'If we say we have no sin, we deceive ourselves, and the truth is not in us. If we confess our sins, God is faithful and just, and will forgive us our sins and cleanse us from all unrighteousness.'

The simplification is obvious. Acknowledgement that our sins are manifold and that they are wicked is subsumed under the single word 'confess'; the possibility that we might dissemble about them, or cover our transgressions with some other kind of cloak before our father's gaze, is crisply summated in 'if . . . we deceive ourselves'; and all reference to humility, lowliness, and penitence and obedience is swept clean away – it must be presumed that they are of subsidiary importance, or can be taken for granted, or are catered for elsewhere. So much for preparation. When it comes to our actual confession the 'simplifying' procedure is equally evident and radical, but it brings strange things in its wake. In the 1662 Prayer Book the General Confession opens expansively:

> Almighty and most merciful Father, we have erred and strayed from thy ways like lost sheep, We have followed too much the devices and desires of our own hearts, We have offended against thy holy laws, We have left undone those things which we ought to have done, And we have done those things which we ought not to have done, And there is no health in us. . . .

The effect of that is inclusive and relentless. We admit that we have offended in a wide variety of ways, we are lawbreakers, lost in error, and diseased. Series 3 shortens the rhythms, and appears to summarise the categories more crisply:

> Almighty God, our heavenly Father,
> we have sinned against you and against our fellow men,
> in thought and word and deed,
> in the evil we have done
> and in the good we have not done,
> through ignorance, through weakness,
> through our own deliberate fault. . .

Yet this apparent simplification has actually brought about a radical restatement of doctrine. 1662, for all its inclusiveness, says nothing about the possibility of sinning 'against our fellow men'. Sin has traditionally been thought of as 'the purposeful disobedience of a creature to the known will of God', it is not so much a moral evil as a fundamentally theological conception. 1662 is God-directed – we have offended against *thy* holy laws – whereas Series 3 has bifurcated the possibility of peccancy. More than that, it has introduced a wholly new way of sinning. We can now sin 'through ignorance', an enticing possibility which Cranmer and his predecessors seemingly overlooked. A member of the Anglican Liturgical Commission once privately explained this as justified by the words from the Cross 'Father, forgive them, for they know not what they do' and exemplified the type of error by those architects and planners who designed high-rise flats. It is not for a humble literary critic to query this new dogma, nor to err and stray like a very lost sheep in the trackless pastures of professional theologians, but he may perhaps be permitted to observe that the process of revising the material of public worship in the interests of ease of understanding may bring about radical changes in the basic doctrines of the Christian faith, obtained without consent of the voting majority. When you take away some of the bricks to let the air in there is a danger that the whole house will collapse around your ears. Simplification is not the simple process it might seem.

One of the concomitant difficulties resides in the fact that a liturgy is not just 'words on a page'. The words are designed to be spoken aloud by all sorts and conditions of men – and women, and children. The place of performance bears certain analogies with a theatre, the processes of public worship are, in the deepest and most serious sense, dramatic. The complex significance of this is shrewdly brought out in a recently-published novel. Alice Thomas Ellis, in *The Sin Eater*, a book which is by no means exclusively concerned with sin, gives one of her characters, a lapsed Roman Catholic, these words:

> There has always been a hint of catering about the Mass, but previously the priest had the dignity of a master chef busying himself with his *specialité*. Now he seems like a singing waiter in charge of an inadequate buffet.

The observation is brutal but enlightening. The priest at the Holy Table is to some extent acting a part, or, to be more precise, performing a role which is a complex of many parts. He is in some sense the representative figure of the tribe, officiating at the sacrificial altar, he is the father at the family dinner table, he is the chairman of the meeting, he is the *chef de cuisine* and head waiter in one. The term 'priest', which the 1662 Book of Common Prayer uses exclusively, has somehow been felt for centuries to cover all these aspects of his function satisfactorily. The Liturgical Commission took a very important step when they renamed him 'the president'. They changed his role. A 'president' cannot stand at an altar (or at least, such a president would have no precedent), a father is not the 'president' of his family, and a president is not a chef. How can the man who officiates at the Series 3 Holy Communion interpret his role? The name given to him, subtly reinforced by the movements he is directed to make and the positions he is told to adopt, points to a performance as chairman at a committee meeting. This is a typical modern role, well understood by members of liturgical commissions, and the opening exchanges (the opening lines in any play are of crucial importance) set the scene:

> The Lord be with you.
> And also with you.

This belongs not to the religious register of dramatic language but to a recognisable type of sociological interaction: it is the equivalent of 'Good morning, children, good morning, Miss' or 'Good afternoon, ladies and gentlemen, the first item on the agenda. . .'. The Eucharist, which used to carry echoes of Jewish sacrificial altars in the open air, and the intensities of the long, European dramatic tradition, and the simplicities of the family supper, has now been modernised, civilised, and redesigned for performance in a company board room. Has it been improved?

The task facing anyone who offers to simplify and 'translate into modern English' one of the great literary masterpieces of the English past is insuperable. The present state of the language prohibits it. But it is not difficult to attempt. Consider, for example, the speech of Othello before the Duke of Venice and his Senators in Act I, scene iii of Shakespeare's play. It begins:

> Most potent, grave, and reverend signors,
> My very noble and approv'd good masters:
> That I have ta'en away this old man's daughter,
> It is most true: true, I have married her,
> The very head and front of my offending
> Hath this extent, no more.

Even though nearly every word in this passage is in current use in contemporary speech this is not 'modern English'. And we do not have Dukes of Venice listening to African mercenaries. But it is easy to translate. If we pick up the hint in 'Senators' we might imagine an American General testifying before a Senate Committee and rewrite Othello's speech in an appropriate idiom:

> Mr Chairman, gentlemen. May I say that I fully recognise your authority in this place, and the gravity of the occasion. It is true that I have taken this distinguished Senator's daughter away from him. Indeed, I have married her. That is the full extent of my offence.

That communicates the sense, and sacrifices the poetry. And it would be impossible for any writer now living to match the poetry while translating the sense into modern English. One need not reach back so far as Shakespeare to enforce the point. Henry Francis

Lyte's famous hymn 'Abide with me' could be modernised on the grounds that words like 'abide' and 'eventide' are archaisms, and that 'comforts' has accreted meanings and shifted semantically since the nineteenth century. A contemporary 'Series 3' version could be made without difficulty:

> Stay with me; evening approaches rapidly,
> The darkness gets deeper. Lord, stay with me.
> When other friends fail me and social security is denied
> Friend of the friendless, please stay with me.

This is not a simple mockery. The point is that such 'translation' is easy to do, but impossible to do well. The English language, as it is at present spoken and written, has no available 'religious register' for the moderniser to use. It is perhaps significant that there is no great evidence of public demand for stylistic up-dating of H. F. Lyte or Shakespeare. Audiences at Wembley and Stratford-upon-Avon seem well content with the originals. One wonders whether the average, middle-of-the-road churchgoer really desperately wanted his Prayer Book brought up to date.

This is not to say that liturgical revision should be banned. On the contrary, every attempt should continually be made by as wide a variety of people as possible to 'make it new'. The campaign which has been waged over the past decade has been fought on too narrow a front. Perhaps from want of eager volunteers the task has devolved upon clergy and laity not specifically trained for the literary task, none of whom is in the front rank of contemporary creative writers. They have 'consulted', of course, and sought advice, comment and criticism. But this very fact is itself evidence of failure. Milton, when he brought the book of Genesis up to date, never submitted his manuscript to a panel of trusted literary advisers – as the translators of the New English Bible did. There was one, single, great creative act and the result was *Paradise Lost*. Well might we say 'Milton, thou shouldst be living at this hour'. The fact is, he is not, nor is there any evidence of any remotely comparable genius on the contemporary literary scene. If there were, he would have to make a poetic language, as Milton did, which would again express the basic truths, doctrines, dogmas and forms of worship at present enshrined in the Book of Common Prayer. It is one man's work. A language cannot emerge from the majority decisions of a committee.

But the English-speaking world cannot simply sit back and wait for the nativity of a latter-day Milton. New forms of worship, fresh approaches to liturgy, should be devised continuously and by all manner of men. Christian poets should labour in this vineyard, but so should Christian journalists, novelists, dramatists, advertising men, lawyers, politicians, civil servants, company directors, and all who are personally and professionally concerned with the power and the glory of the spoken word. Actors and actresses, not panels of trusted literary advisers, are the best critics of experimental liturgies. Dame Flora Robson is a better judge of a prayer designed for public use than any number of university professors. Instead of trying to replace The Book of Common Prayer with something rather like it the Anglican Communion should be expanding and exploring new possibilities, learning from anthropologists and sociologists about the deep structures of ritual, venturing boldly into areas of language hitherto deemed unsuitable for the expression of religious truth and feeling. Our present discontents stem from the fact that liturgical revision has homed in on committee-language, the bureaucrat's idiolect, the consensus-dominated speech of administrative life as the answer to all its problems. It is not. It may be the dominant speech-style of our time in Western Europe and the United States, but it has never generated the vocabulary, rhythms and rhetoric necessary for public worship. It can never rest easy in the presence of imagery and symbolism because these are, of their very nature, imprecise and suggestive, likening things to one another, not equating them intellectually and scientifically.

The basic error in liturgical revision has been the attempt to converge on a single text rather than diverging into a multiplicity. Series 3 has foundered on the rock of the highest common factor. No one in his senses would try (especially by setting up a committee) to produce a generally acceptable, single, modernised text of Shakespeare for performance in the theatre. But the present practice of dramatists faced with the challenge of Shakespeare to the present day may afford a clue to liturgical scholars of the future. Contemporary dramatists have not focussed minutely on Shakespeare's language, they have rewritten whole plays. Brecht took *Coriolanus* and rewrote it in contemporary terms. Edward Bond took *King Lear* as the basis for his own analysis of the ills of society. Tom Stoppard took characters and incidents from *Hamlet* and reassembled them in *Rosencrantz and Guildenstern are dead*, using Shakespeare's words when they suited his purpose and writing his own dialogue when they did not. *Kiss me Kate* and *West Side Story* show how far and how acceptably writers are prepared to go in adapting Shakespearean comedy and tragedy for new purposes. Such adaptations and experiments are often exciting and revealing. But they leave the great originals untouched. The regular, world-wide performance of

Shakespeare's original texts continues like a great river which is only fed and swollen by these tributaries.

The Book of Common Prayer is at present irreplaceable. The time is not ripe, and the language is not fit. It was composed when English was at a particularly rich and expressive state of its development, and, as W. H. Auden said, 'why spit on your luck?'. It would be blind folly to displace it as the central text for the conduct of public worship in the Church of England. Liturgical revision should go on continuously and restlessly, but we should measure our attempts, in our very different language, against Thomas Cranmer's monumental achievement and realise how far we fall short. We should be prepared to say with T. S. Eliot, the greatest poet of the twentieth century, and a religious poet: 'That was a way of putting it – not very satisfactory.' But we must go on producing new liturgies all the time, realising as he did that

Words strain,
Crack and sometimes break, under the burden,
Under the tension, slip, slide, perish,
Decay with imprecision, will not stay in place,
Will not stay still.

Eliot's insight applies to Cranmer's liturgy as it does to everything else. The Book of Common Prayer is not immutable and eternal, but we have produced nothing yet which is remotely capable of replacing it. The struggle to do so goes on.

Leaving one still with the intolerable wrestle
With words and meanings.

74

. . .
The Book of Common Prayer we knew
Was that of 1662:
Though with-it sermons may be well,
Liturgical reforms are hell. . . .

Though I suspect the term is crap,
If there *is* a Generation Gap,
Who is to blame? Those, old or young,
Who will not learn their Mother-Tongue.

W. H. AUDEN
from 'Doggerel by a Senior Citizen'

The new religious English:
A form of unbelief of the day
ANDOR GOMME

What is religious language for? To enable us to express our religious beliefs, opinions, sentiments – in short, our religious experience? But this will not do; for a belief or an idea cannot identify itself outside of *some* language, cannot really be said to exist until it has found expression. Perhaps, then, religious language exists to *define* our religious experience, and by extension to give the possibility of understanding it: a medium in which we can identify and explore experiences of a particular kind. But this formula still supposes an experience in principle separable from its 'expression'. Consider the same question asked of the language of mathematics: what is it for? Not just to allow the mathematician to talk mathematics with his fellows: its prime function is to make mathematics possible; mathematicians make a language in order to enable them to do mathematics, an activity inconceivable without its language. I suggest that we may say likewise that religious language is needed so that we may do religion; or, since that phrase is intolerable, so that we may be religious. But why is it intolerable? Not just as an ugly neologism; nor, certainly, because religion is not characteristically active. Rather because it suggests that religion is just one activity among others to be picked up and put down at choice. But the activeness of religion is an expression of the continuing religious life, of *being* religious. A very important point about religious experience is that, unlike pain or contentment, it is not a special kind or tone of experience which comes every now and again in special circumstances, but that it qualifies all experience of whatever kind. Religious language makes religious experience possible: it is a precondition of whatever understanding the religious person can have of the world and of whatever he can do in it.

This position does not imply that religious language is logically prior to religion itself; it is not nominalist, for religion is guaranteed not by human experience but by God himself. We must have no other gods before him, not because they might distract us from him, but simply because he is the Lord our God. In a religious situation God is always the conceptual subject: 'herein is love, not that we

75

loved God, but that he loved us' (I John 4:10) – a truth heedlessly
thrown away by a fuzzy blurring of the Greek and the intrusion of
a wholly unjustified personal pronoun in both the Jerusalem Bible
('this is the love I mean') and the New English ('the love I spoke
of'). John isn't singling out one love among others: he has said
unequivocally that God is love, and now he tells us what love is,
and that we are always the recipients. But our understanding of the
substantial reality of God's love *is* dependent on the language we
have to realise, to reify it.

To ask how far the actual language available to us limits and
influences the quality of our religious experience is a matter of
importance, therefore. The 'actual language available' to very many
English Christians has recently suffered a major change through the
widespread use of new translations of the Bible and new English
versions of the liturgy. The Jerusalem Bible is now used in almost
all English Catholic churches; the New English has not yet taken
over the Church of England so completely, thanks to the tenacity
of affection for the Authorised Version, but it is gaining ground.
People, through apprehensiveness of the unfamiliar, will tend to
turn to what looks more like the rest of their language. How far our
experience has been affected must obviously be a speculation; but
some degree of familiarity with the new texts gives us an acquaintance with their linguistic habits and the attitudes to religious belief
which they reveal.

'How shall men meditate in that, which they cannot understand?
How shall they understand that which is kept close in an unknowen
tongue? as it is written, Except that I know the power of the voyce,
I shall be to him that speaketh, a Barbarian, and he that speaketh,
shall be a Barbarian to me.' All modern translators contend that the
language of the 1611 Bible (the quotation comes from the Preface
to the Reader) and even of the Revised Version is to most Englishmen now almost as unknowen a tongue as Greek and Latin, out of
which it was the concern of the godly-learned to translate the Scriptures 'for the behoofe and edifying of the unlearned which hungred
and thirsted after Righteousnesse, and had soules to be saved aswell
as they.' The strangeness of the idiom of the Authorised Version
today has been much exaggerated. Certainly it contains archaic
words and usages, and more importantly its rhythms are often
difficult for readers who have no other acquaintance with early
seventeenth-century English. This difficulty is a real one: it is an
aspect of the whole style of the Authorised Version which expresses

the translators' instinct for what they were about. The 'vulgar' tongue into which the Bible was translated in the succession of versions culminating in 1611 was not ordinary speech; it wasn't even the ordinary literary English of the day insofar as there was such a thing. What the translators from Wyclif onwards did was to create a religious language within English: not a technical jargon like the language of biochemistry, say, but still a special creation for a special purpose: a language in which it was possible to think and talk about God.

Why should we be surprised that this language is often strange and sometimes difficult? It is not easy to read the truth about God: one cannot expect to do it in the language proper for ordinary events of the day; for the truth about God is not ordinary in this sense. To suppose that it can be written even in a refined version of the language we are used to in newspapers is to turn the word of God to genteel journalism, and his mystery and strangeness to what is merely odd or unusual.

> Behold, I shew you a mystery; We shall not all sleep, but we shall all be changed, in a moment, in the twinkling of an eye, at the last trump: for the trumpet shall sound, and the dead shall be raised incorruptible, and we shall be changed.
>
> (I Cor. 15:51–2)

Isn't that an amazing, a stunning announcement – amazing in its assertion of the unimaginable power of God? does it not change the whole world for believers? is it something we could ever become *used to*? and can we not feel the triumphant strangeness of what Paul tells us in the exultant rhythm of the English, in the way in which an ordinary word such as 'sleep' or 'changed' is changed indeed, opening a glimpse into the umplumbable depths of the mystery, which is not just something puzzling in the trivial modern sense of the word, but the positive infinitude of God? And what does the Jerusalem Bible give us in place of this matchless promise?

> I will tell you something that has been secret: that we are not all going to die, but we shall all be changed. This will be instantaneous, in the twinkling of an eye, when the last trumpet sounds. It will sound, and the dead will be raised, imperishable, and we shall be changed as well, because . . .

But who will credit explanations after that? There is no new life here: it is the world of a minor government official leaking something to the press. (Not much of a leak either, for Paul has let the 'secret' out long before and has imagined someone asking 'How are dead people raised, and what sort of body do they have when they come back?' These are stupid questions, he is supposed to comment (v. 36), but in the world whose language is that of the Jerusalem Bible they are on the contrary sensible and apt; the real Paul says nothing about them.) And since what he leaks *is* so strange, so odd, it becomes in consequence simply incredible – a conjuring, or worse a confidence, trick; it is impossible to think of its being taken seriously. (The Jerusalem people don't, if one is to judge by the dismal slipshod chumminess with which, a verse before, the great prophecy is ushered in: 'Or else, brothers, put it this way . . .') Probably there are many who, sensible that the new version comes off badly in the comparison, may nevertheless feel that what it lacks is a certain grandeur of manner, a flourish of literary style, even though, as so often, it can be shown that the language of the Authorised Version is much sparer and more economical, every word charged with meaning. It cannot be denied that the writer who lets the wonderful moment trail away so hopelessly with 'as well' tacked on at the end, has a wretched ear for how English sentences mean; he goes pseudo-scientific with 'instantaneous' but lamely re-uses 'the twinkling of an eye', which in the context sounds just quaint; and he has no notion of why 'imperishable' is here so weak a substitute for 'incorruptible'. But the fundamental difference between the two passages is not comprehended in what most people would think of as literary skill at all: it is a matter of belief. As Ian Robinson says, 'any religious language is *ipso facto* ruined by the failure of the belief which makes it meaningful – and which it allows to be meaningful' (*The Survival of English*, 1973, p 64). The failure of the language marks something more profound.

'But', it will be exclaimed, 'we are dealing with a translation, and the question we must ask is how accurately it renders the original: is the thrill of Paul's vision there in the Greek?' And what if it were not? Would it not then be a great discovery of the old translators? Robinson (p 45) makes an essential point in speaking of Tyndale, that his 'earnest effort to be true to the meaning of the original . . . was inseparable from his urgent knowledge of his mission to speak the word of God in English, so that he who seeks may find.' Is it possible to believe in any such mission in this passage from the Jerusalem Bible? Can one read it in a way which will prevent its sounding trivial? One cannot. But if what one writes is trivial, it cannot be the word of God. To try to speak the word of God anew in any language, whether one is translating or not, demands always a sense of its authority, which, if it cannot raise the language to the level of belief, will sink it to the banal and incredible. In fact Paul's

Greek is unmannered, using no unusual words; but the moment's immense importance for him is apparent in the pulsing urgency of his short clauses, so precisely rendered in the English of 1611: if it was so urgent a matter for Paul then he must have been gripped by the need to *create* a language of belief out of the ordinary Greek which he shared with those to whom he was writing. Consider only that word μυστήριον, which the Jerusalem reduces to 'something that has been secret'. The Greek word does have this sense, of what was hidden, reserved for initiates; and the rites with which it had long been associated were by this time threadbare: the word itself was tired. But Paul had no other and so must wrest it out of decay to express the unfathomable mystery of God's new covenant with the world. This was only possible – he could only make it a part of a new religious language – because he believed passionately in the mystery. The evidence of the new translations is that this is a belief we no longer hold.

Belief will atrophy without a language of belief. But the assumption of the need for – or even the possibility of – a religious language seems to be counter to the presuppositions, as to the practice, of modern translators. So, for instance, I judge from the editor's foreword to the Reader's Edition of the Jerusalem Bible, whose original aim was

> to serve two pressing needs facing the Church, the need to keep abreast of the times and the need to deepen theological thought. This double programme was carried out by translating the ancient texts into the language we use today, and by providing notes to the text which were neither sectarian nor superficial . . . the English version was offered as an entirely faithful rendering of the original texts which [were] . . . adopted in the light of the most recent researches in the fields of history, archaeology and literary criticism. With the text, the Standard Edition presented the full explanatory notes that would enable any student to confirm for himself the interpretations that were adopted, to appreciate the theological implications drawn from them, and to understand the complex relations between the different parts of the Bible.
>
> However the Bible is not only for students undergoing a formal course of study, and there has been an immediate demand for an edition of the Jerusalem Bible which would bring the modern clarity of the text before the ordinary reader . . . the brief Introductions and Notes are here only to help the ordinary reader to understand what he is reading [only that!] and do not assume in

him any wide literary, historical or theological knowledge or interests.

This seems to me to represent an amazing surrender. Why should a new translation of the Bible be ushered in so apologetically, disguised as a curious old document of anthropological, 'non-sectarian' interest to students? The committee has, it seems, heard of historical criticism and been rather winded by it; so the new Bible's credentials are wholly defensive. But if Christianity is now simply fighting a rearguard action to cover the end of a permanent retreat, it is time to be honest and give up. Even the 'ordinary reader', for whom as an afterthought it was realised that copies might be made available, is a weird kind of blank without 'literary, historical or theological knowledge or interests' – or religious ones either. Why should such a reader pick up any Bible at all? and if he did, why should he be impressed by one which begins by giving away its foundations? I am ready to believe in the need to deepen theological thought; but the Bible is not first of all a theological source-book, it is the prime source of Christian experience: any withdrawal from that position is a surrender of the ground of concern for it. If that concern is not religious, then the Bible is only one of many historical documents in the wayward chronicles of men.

That other pressing need announced in the foreword – that the Church should 'keep abreast of the times' – seems at first to make a strange bedfellow for the deepening of theological thought. But the same defensive apologetic is at work in both. The motive is transparent: has not the Church been continuously losing ground through the whole of this century, and is not one main cause its out-of-date image? But to keep abreast of the times is to ally oneself with the *merely* temporal: that which is only living can only die, and that which is only passing is in a moment gone, and the place thereof shall know it no more. Of course the Church must speak in a language in which ordinary people can be brought to approach God (for how indeed shall men meditate in that which they cannot understand?), and must be intimately concerned with the real urgencies of the present: those things which actually do press hardly on people can be ignored only at the peril of being thought to be without anything to offer in answer to cries of pain and need. But to answer merely in terms of present imagery is to limit the word of God to what present imagery can supply – a woeful limitation in times like our own, when the common language is so bloodless.

An obvious result of such a policy is that many of the clichés in which the Jerusalem Bible abounds were born dated. The habit of cliché is evidence of banality and shallowness of mind: thus the glaring howler at the start of Psalm 69 is soon revealed as part of a deep ignorance of how language works. Here are the first six verses according to Jerusalem:

> Save me, God! The water
> is already up to my neck!

> I am sinking in the deepest swamp,
> there is no foothold;
> I have stepped into deep water
> and the waves are washing over me.

> Worn out with calling, my throat is hoarse,
> my eyes are strained, looking for my God.

> More people hate me for no reason
> than I have hairs on my head,
> more are groundlessly hostile
> than I have hair to show.
> (They ask me to give back what I never took.)

> God, you know how foolish I have been,
> my offences are not hidden from you;

> but let those who hope in you not blush for me,
> Yahweh Sabaoth!
> Let those who seek you not be ashamed of me,
> God of Israel!

If one tries the experiment of reading this passage aloud, certain 'surface' faults are immediately apparent, most noticeably that it is so short-winded – a succession of clauses, virtually identical in such rhythm as they have, too repetitive to be brief with the breathlessness of urgent peril. In v. 4 the repetition becomes verbal, a piece of elegant variation to no purpose; and David's enemies are mightily polite that they should *ask* him to give back. V.5 gives momentarily the shocking impression that the name of God is there as an oath; and v.6 is grammatically – and hence semantically – ambiguous: one cannot tell *from this text* whether the second 'not' goes with what precedes or with what follows it. The muddled and shoddy English shows that the translator has no idea what the trouble is about: it is not only David who has stepped into deeper water than he can cope with. But what kind of water is it? The language *seems* to be insistently literal (though someone who was really thinking about his choice of words might have reflected that waves aren't characteristic of swamps): a man, it seems, has actually fallen into a marsh; this impression is strong enough to overwhelm v.3, so that we have the ridiculous situation of the struggling man peering through the gloom hoping for a literal sight of God. When, then, we come to his confession of folly and sinfulness in v.5, there seems to be no connexion with what has gone before (except for an obviously unintentional one). If the translator thinks of the water and the swamp as a metaphor, the reader of the Jerusalem text is simply left guessing what they might be a metaphor of.

The Authorised Version is as follows:

> Save me, O God;
> For the waters are come in unto my soul.
> I sink in deep mire, where there is no standing:
> I am come into deep waters, where the floods overflow me.
> I am weary of my crying: my throat is dried:
> Mine eyes fail while I wait for my God.
> They that hate me without a cause are more than the hairs of mine head:
> They that would destroy me, being mine enemies wrongfully, are mighty:
> Then I restored that which I took not away.
> O God, thou knowest my foolishness;
> And my sins are not hid from thee.
> Let not them that wait on thee, O Lord God of hosts, be ashamed for my sake:
> Let not those that seek thee be confounded for my sake, O God of Israel.

From the very first we know what we are about. Though the swamp is no longer literal, the pressure of the waters is much more urgent: no longer is David floundering in a marsh from which he might be pulled out if only someone turned his way: these waters have not merely come up to his neck, but into his soul, and it's no joke waiting for God in *that* plight: how could he not go blind with the awful separation? The blindness *is* the separation. The words do not lose their literal strength because the metaphor is overt: on the contrary, the agony is all the intenser for the physical weight of the imagery. What then has happened to lead the new translator into such a blunder? Is it that he has himself no experience of the kind of peril when it *really matters* that one has lost one's foothold? or is it that he does not trust his readers to sense that it is a religious situation at all? Why, after all, should God pay any attention to the directionless grumbling that the Jerusalem David goes in for? (At the start of the following psalm, the question becomes even more pressing, with the grotesquely petulant tone he adopts: 'Oh come and rescue me, God, Yahweh come quickly and help me.') This is perhaps the place to say briefly that the Jerusalem's attempt to localise Yahweh into an English word ought to have been seen to be impossible from the start. We can be thankful that Yahweh has so far not invaded the liturgy, for the word remains unalterably alien and distractingly intrusive. What could be worse or more meaningless than the opening of the 91st Psalm?

> If you live in the shelter of Elyon
> and make your home in the shadow of Shaddai,
> you can say to Yahweh, 'My refuge, my fortress,
> my God in whom I trust!'

And if you don't, what then? The effect of the hypothetical is total disaster (and the shadow of Shaddai must have been an irresistible trouvaille). A footnote records that 'four names for God are used in this strophe: Elyon, Shaddai, Yahweh and Elohim. They can be rendered, the Most High, the God of heaven, the Lord, God.' If they can be so rendered (virtually as in the A.V.!) why are they not? This isn't even an attempt to write English. (Surely, too, the lonely splendour of the revelation of the name Jehovah (Exodus 6:3) is simply wrecked by the freedom with which it is bandied about in the rest of the Old Testament? This again is, I should say, a discovery of the old translation.) 'Hades' which in several places does duty for 'hell' (e.g., Luke 16:23 where Dives looks up from 'his torment in Hades') ought likewise to have been proscribed. To those who know anything of classical mythology the associations of the word will be slightly comic where they are not a distracting irrelevance; those who do not will be just bemused. The translators ought to have seen that ᾅδης was simply a device used by the writers of the Greek testament to adapt an old word to a concept new to the language: it is as foreign to modern English as Yahweh; but it seems that the new men don't wish too often to mention hell to ears polite.

The tendency to withdraw into cliché always betrays a failure in perception: it attempts to draw on the secondhand, but the language is a counterfeit, which can never be made to realise value. It might seem that in translating one is always working at second hand, trying for 'an entirely faithful rendering of the original texts'. Two major and linked fallacies are implied by this formula: first, that ideally there would be an exact one-to-one correspondence between original and translation; but no language is reducible without remainder to another, because language is a product and definition of a culture. Secondly, that at any given time any given language would be adequate as a vehicle for translating another and realising its perceptions anew. In the two centuries before 1611, a language was created which made it possible to render in English with astonishing accuracy the perceptions and – I will hazard – the impulses of the Hebrew and Greek. That there were technical imperfections is doubtless true; and of course there is always one last division which is unbridgeable, which is what we mean by saying that English is a different language from Hebrew or Greek. But the language of the Authorised Version proved itself – uniquely in the history of English – as fully up to its task as is humanly possible: an astounding task after all – to speak the word of God. It was not, to repeat an essential point, the ordinary language of the day, though it *was* contemporary English. The notion that we can simply take up 'the language we use today' and find it adequate to the task of *any* translation has no foundation at all. The language of Shakespeare's time was not itself adequate, and a great effort of creation had gone into its making. What for example if the language we use today has not words for some things that the originals talk about? How can the old text be 'preserved' in a language which seems to be without the power of redefining essential concepts in the religion preached by Christ and the prophets? If our belief in righteousness and in sin is so weak that we cannot use the words without embarrassment, we are likely to make a poor show of translating the Bible. There is, alas, altogether too much evidence now to doubt that the beliefs embodied in the language we use today are not up to the tremendous task. 'The modern clarity of the text', which the Jerusalem foreword quaintly talks of, is a thoroughly modern muddle about what we believe. (Is the clarity supposed to be something new to the modern translation, or is it a new kind of clarity, or does the editor after all only mean the clarity of the modern text?)

What, however, do we understand by 'an entirely faithful rendering'? Much of the argument which accompanied the appearance of the modern Bibles concentrated on the supposed inaccuracies of the old versions, which had been shown up by 'recent researches in the fields of history, archaeology and literary criticism'. The old translators had got a number of things fairly grossly wrong (not their fault, poor chaps – they didn't have the blessings of modern machinery), and the new scholarship would put all to rights. But inaccuracies of translation can only be corrected within a particular language; and a language only exists within a culture which creates, uses and receives it. There is no such thing as accuracy in the abstract. In the general introduction to the Jerusalem Bible it was said that 'the first duty of a translator is to convey as clearly as he can what the original author wrote'. But the only way to do that is to repeat the original author's words: any translation is a reinterpretation, because languages differ and because they are not merely collections of words and grammatical rules which can be paired off against one another in parallel columns. Accuracy is in fact always a three-term relationship, involving in addition to the original and the translation, the receptivity and expectations of the audience (which includes the translator himself); or to put it another way, what the language can do at any given moment. Even at an elementary level, though, the claims to accuracy of the new versions look shabby, as one can on occasion discover without recourse to the original, simply because the language of the translation betrays itself. At Jeremiah 17:9, where the Authorised Version gives us a grim and stark view of the human heart as 'deceitful above all things, and desperately wicked', the Jerusalem has 'the heart is more devious than any other thing, perverse too'. The first phrase suggests the quite irrelevant question of what other things Jeremiah might have been comparing it with, whereas the essential point, which the Authorised catches exactly, is the heart's endless deceptiveness (not only is it the most deceitful of all things, but its essential nature is to deceive) the second, with its modish 'perverse' for the straightforward and hard-hitting 'wicked', is simply flippant, an apparent afterthought which dismisses the subject in an offhand, idle way. It cannot be right as a translation of Jeremiah's minatory outburst, for what could possibly be the point of adding the subsidiary 'perverse' to the already damning 'devious'? Another kind of flippancy occurs often in Job, for example at the opening of chapter 40, where the Authorised and still more brilliantly the Revised Version, bring Job and his reader to their knees: 'Shall he that cavilleth contend with the Almighty? He that argueth with God, let him answer it.' But the Jerusalem's God is a cynical tease: 'Is Shaddai's opponent willing to give in? Has God's critic thought up an answer?' Oddly enough Job replies to this taunting with 'My words have been frivolous'. But the frivolity at this point is not Job's.

Often the attempt to find new words simply results in new mystification. In Psalm 49, v.4, the Authorised Version gives

I will incline mine ear to a parable;
I will open my dark saying upon the harp.

Decidedly cryptic for a twentieth-century reader (and perhaps for
a seventeenth-century one): the dark saying is dark indeed. But how
does the Jerusalem help?

> I turn my attention to a proverb
> and set my solution to the harp.

'Turn my attention' has a relaxed, supercilious casualness which is
wholly inappropriate; and for the rest the phrasing suggests that the
'solution', which the psalmist for some reason wants to *set* to music,
is to some unspecified problem posed by the proverb. But what?
This line cannot communicate. (It is, however, a little better than
another popular current version which announces 'I will solve my
problem on the harp' as if it were an abacus. The RSV even talks
of solving 'my riddle': why should the psalmist be bothering his
head over riddles?)

Sorting the sense out is not always straightforward; and many
readers familiar with older versions will have gone to the new ones
for help with a difficult passage. There is a famous theological crux
in Hebrews (6:4–6) about the sin against the Holy Ghost – and not
only a theological one: it has caused anxious and unresolved heart-
searchings to many seeking to know what is this sin which it is
impossible to repent. The AV hints, but is not explicit:

> it is impossible for those who were once enlightened, and have
> tasted of the heavenly gift, and were made partners of the Holy
> Ghost, and have tasted the good word of God, and the powers of
> the world to come, if they shall fall away, to renew them again to
> repentance; seeing they crucify to themselves the Son of God
> afresh, and put him to an open shame.

Plainly this is against backsliding; but are we not enjoined to forgive
until seventy times seven times? and shall not our Father in Heaven
do the same? Alas the Jerusalem, turning the whole passage into a
looser contemporary idiom, puts a new, and demonstrably unjusti-
fiable, stumbling-block before the blind. The change may seem
insignificant, but it is crucial: it lies in a change of tense in the last
clause:

> As for those people who were once brought into the light, and
> tasted the gift from heaven, and received a share of the Holy
> Spirit, and appreciated the good message of God and the powers
> of the world to come and yet in spite of this have fallen away –
> it is impossible for them to be renewed a second time. They

cannot be repentant if they have wilfully crucified the Son of God and openly mocked him.

Why can they not? There is no explanation in the new version which at this point gravely and improperly departs from the Greek. As in the Authorised and Revised versions, the Greek is a single continuous sentence: it consists of a string of participles and could be literally and awkwardly rendered thus: 'it is impossible to those once enlightened [or instructed], having tasted the heavenly gift, and having become sharers in the Holy Spirit, and having tasted the good [or beautiful] word of God and the powers of eternity to come, and having fallen aside, to renew them again to repentance, recrucifying for themselves the Son of God and putting him to shame.' The technical point is that all the Greek participles are aorist (and thus imply single actions) until the last two, which are present and imply by contrast a continuing state: i.e., *so long as* they recrucify and mock, repentance is impossible. Whether this is good modern theology I don't know, but something like it is what the Greek means, and the slack language of the Jerusalem (which rules out this reading by its careless paraphrase) must be recorded as a mistranslation in the most elementary sense – and one which has power to cause groundless and unprofitable pain. So much for the entirely faithful rendering of the original.

There is surely no deep theological thinking behind such an error as this: even though it forces a wholly new interpretation on to the text, no more sinister intention than lies behind the failure to align quotations in the New Testament with their original appearances in the Old. Sometimes, however, I suspect the forcing of a theological point. In place of the familiar 'they twain shall be one flesh' (Matt. 19:5) the Jerusalem has 'the two become one body'. Body? Plainly in any literal sense they don't, and the word makes the metaphor much harder to grasp. Moreover the evangelist's word is σάρξ, not σῶμα which is kept back for Christ's consecration of the Eucharist. This too is a case of simple mistranslation; but it may not be quite innocent. At least it shows how the sort of connexion which one may *believe* Christ to be hinting at can twist the translation of what he actually said.

Is there anything behind the seemingly aimless tinkerings that are so common? Towards the end of the first Epistle to the Thessalonians Paul makes a fine-spirited call to his people. The AV keeps especially close to the Greek.

Now we exhort you, brethren, warn them that are unruly, comfort the feebleminded, support the weak, be patient toward all men.

> See that none render evil for evil unto any man; but ever follow
> that which is good, both among yourselves, and to all men.
> Rejoice evermore. Pray without ceasing. In every thing give
> thanks; for this is the will of God in Christ concerning you. (I
> Thess. 5:14–18)

The intention is certain, the injunctions firm, but delivered with
respect for those addressed. The effect in the Jerusalem is extremely
different:

> And this is what we ask you to do, brothers: warn the idlers, give
> courage to those who are apprehensive, care for the weak and be
> patient with everyone. Make sure that people do not try to take
> revenge; you must all think of what is best for each other and for
> the community. Be happy at all times; pray constantly; and for
> all things give thanks to God, because this is what God expects
> you to do in Christ Jesus.

Can anyone believe that this is St Paul speaking? No governess
could do better. Everything is weakened: 'exhort' becomes 'ask';
the 'unruly' are made into 'idlers'; 'see that none render evil for
evil' gives place to 'make sure that people do not try to take revenge'
(as if anyway they were not strong enough to succeed); worst of all
'the will of God' degenerates into 'what God expects you to do'.
Expects indeed. What can this tentative, unconfident Paul be
expecting of his people? No wonder that in his attempt to cheer
them up the best he can offer is a wish for their happiness. What
is truly alarming is that the only possible explanation is that the
translator cannot see any difference in meaning between 'Rejoice'
and 'Be happy': rejoicing is outside his vocabulary, because he
doesn't know what it is to rejoice. (And if that is true of him, what
hope for his readers who are simply denied the chance to know
what Paul said?) He thinks that 'constantly' (which in context will
be understood to mean no more than 'often') will do for Paul's
ἀδιαλείπτως, because he cannot believe that Paul was really requiring us to pray without ceasing. But surely Paul meant exactly what
he said: everything we do must be turned into prayer: whatsoever
ye do, do all to the glory of God. And who in such weak-kneed
company will even notice the infelicity of 'you must all think [only
think?] of what is best for each other and for the community'? Paul
is talking about the *good* – which at our peril we must follow, not
only within our 'community' but to all men. It is not too much to
say that all sense of what Paul, a Christian believer, will have
understood by 'the good' has vanished without trace.

The corresponding exhortation in Philippians (4:4–9) is even more miserably feeble and without hope. How could anyone read without embarrassment 'I want you to be happy, always happy in the Lord; I repeat, what I want is your happiness'? (Why *should* he repeat it? has he nothing better to do?) There used to be a popular song which began 'I want to be happy, but I can't be happy till I make you happy too': the Jerusalem is to the marvellous English of the AV what the song is to the marvellous music which Purcell made for the old text: 'Rejoice in the Lord alway, and again I say rejoice' – for the rejoicing is so strong in Paul himself that the call *must* come again. Lest it seem, however, that I deplore the version of our time simply because it cannot match the irresistible beauty of that of 1611, I must repeat that the chief complaint about what the Jerusalem makes of Paul is that it empties him of meaning. 'Let your tolerance be evident to everyone' [but why tolerance? moderation is a positive quality – the NEB even plumps daringly for 'magnanimity'; also to be evident is not the same as to be known]; 'the Lord is very near' [how near? just round the corner? has this man no sense of the ludicrous? the Jerusalem translators haven't, or how could they miss the disgraceful howler at I Thess. 4:16 – 'At the trumpet of God, the voice of the archangel will call out the command and the Lord himself will come down'? Somebody has been going to too many pantos]. 'There is no need to worry; but if there is anything you need [*if?*], pray for it . . . and that peace of God which is so much greater than we can understand' [with such limited understanding who could wonder? the peace Paul talks of is beyond *all* understanding, a part of the unfathomable mystery] 'will guard your hearts and your thoughts, in Christ Jesus. Finally, brothers, fill your minds with everything that is true, everything that is noble, everything that is good and pure, everything that we love and honour, and everything that can be thought virtuous or worthy of praise.' Stuff it all in. The sentence drags its weary, mechanical length along and finally collapses of exhaustion. The real Paul called on his Philippians to rejoice, because he knew the presence of the Lord, who is *at hand*; and just for this he expected them to call on God in everything (not just if there was something they happened to notice the need of – as who should say, 'we need a new washing-up mop, let's pray for it'). The pseudo-Paul of the Jerusalem is a spineless social counsellor, offering synthetic comfort in words which no one could credit: everything is going to be all right, there is no need to worry – Paul's 'last advice' as the passage is aptly headed. The language of Jerusalem Paul is not the language of belief.

What is at the root of this failure to find a new way to speak credibly the language of God? Is it just a failure of nerve, as the modern translation constantly gives the impression of backing away from words which make demands on us and are admittedly not now in very common use? One Sunday in July the Old Testament reading at Mass ended with the following:

> See the days are coming – it is the Lord who speaks – when I will raise a virtuous Branch for David, who will reign as true king and be wise, practising honesty and integrity in the land. In his days Judah will be saved and Israel dwell in confidence. And this is the name he will be called: The Lord-our-Integrity.
>
> (Jer. 23:5–6)

Does the Lord really speak so oddly and in a language so far removed from that that we use today? At the end we were assured with due solemnity, 'This is the word of the Lord'. But it can't be – not because the words are blasphemous or profane, but because they aren't in *any* known language. 'The Lord-our-integrity' is not English, and if not English certainly nothing else. Doubtless the Hebrew is difficult, and the AV may seem no better off: 'this is the name whereby he shall be called, THE LORD OUR RIGHTEOUS- NESS'. Without question the strangeness of the phrase remains. But strangeness – which might be expected here; it is a promise of something wholly new – is not impossibility. I can't fully explain what the phrase means; but I do affirm that *righteousness* can make a sense here which *integrity* cannot. Integrity is an inner virtue: not that we could have it without God's grace, but in our modern language (the original sense of wholeness has now gone from the word) a definition would be internal to the individual: it has its complete usage within an essentially secular context. But righteous- ness not only cannot come to us except through grace: it cannot even be defined without reference to grace, it means nothing without God. So Christ must be the righteous, not just the virtuous, branch: only the Lord could lead us in the paths of righteousness; the paths of virtue make a different and secularised demand – on those faced by 'a gloomy valley' rather than that of the shadow of death.

For a time I believed that 'righteousness' and 'righteous' had been completely expunged from the Jerusalem Bible. I'm glad to find that I was mistaken, but it remains true that constantly, at crucial points for the understanding of our religion, the word is evaded and the concept burked. After the earthquake at the crucifixion the centurion in Luke (23.47) 'glorified God, saying, Certainly this was a righteous man'; but in the Jerusalem no more than a great and good one. Why glorify God for a great man? The centurion's opinion is not final evidence, but the evangelists thought it important enough to bring in at that great moment and must have supposed a connexion between the earthquake and Christ's link with God – i.e., for the centurion, his righteousness. Over and again, in one context and writer after another, the Jerusalem moves away from the idea of righteousness into something with which the modern world is more at ease. A few examples taken at random from the AV with Jerusalem alternatives in brackets:

Prov. 29:2 When the righteous are in authority [virtuous men in power], the people rejoice [are joyful].

Isa. 33:15 He that walketh righteously [acts with integrity] . . . he shall dwell on high [in the heights]. (Which heights? there are many, including that of folly.)

Isa. 57:1–2 The righteous perisheth, and no man layeth it to heart: and merciful men are taken away, none considering that the righteous is taken away from the evil to come. He shall enter into peace . . . [The upright perish and no one cares. Devout men are taken off and no one gives it a thought. Yes, on account of evil the upright man is taken off to enter peace.] (Surely very baffling: what part does evil play in his entering into peace?)

Matt. 5:6 Blessed [happy] are they which do hunger and thirst after righteousness [what is right]: for they shall be filled [satisfied(!)].

Matt. 25:46 These shall go away into everlasting punishment: but the righteous [virtuous] into life eternal.

Luke 16:9 Make to yourselves friends of the mammon of unrighteousness; that, when ye fail, they may receive you into everlasting habitations [use money, tainted as it is, to win you friends, and thus make sure that when it fails you, they will welcome you into the tents of eternity]. (This seems to me a piece of *deliberate* ambiguity: 'the mammon of unrighteousness' is a word-for-word rendering of the Greek; and as Christ a few verses later warns us that we cannot serve God and mammon, we must take his word 'righteousness' seriously. Yet the NEB goes even further and drops all sense of reprobation from the phrase: 'use your worldly wealth to win friends . . .'

Jas. 5:16 The effectual fervent prayer of a righteous man availeth much. [The heart-felt prayer of a good man works very powerfully.]

I John 2:1–2 If any man sin, we have an advocate with the Father,

Jesus Christ the righteous: and he is the propitiation for our sins. [If anyone should (!) sin, we have our advocate with the Father, Jesus Christ, who is just; he is the sacrifice that takes our sins away.] (How? 'propitiation' tells us.)
I John 5:17 All unrighteousness [every kind of wrong-doing] is sin.

Righteousness is not the only casualty; 'soul' is hardly to be counted on:

Prov. 19:16 He that keepeth the commandment keepeth his own soul [is keeper of himself].
Mark 8:36 What shall it profit a man, if he shall gain the whole world, and lose his own soul [ruin his life]?

Likewise 'bless' and 'blessed', as in the Beatitudes which the Jerusalem turns into the felicities with 'happy' throughout, and as at Matt. 16:17: 'Blessed art thou, Simon Bar-jona: for flesh and blood hath not revealed it unto thee, but my Father which is in heaven' [Simon son of Jonah, you are a happy man! Because it was not flesh and blood that revealed this to you but my Father in heaven] – the connexion between the two sentences is now decidedly obscure. At the Last Supper (Matt. 26:26) we learn now not that Jesus blessed the bread, but that he 'said the blessing' – which sounds like a merely ritual grace.

Now if to lose one's soul is no more than to ruin one's life, if to be happy is all we mean by being blessed, if righteousness is simply integrity and virtue brings eternal life, what need have we of religion? Did not Christ in blessing the bread make it *sacred*? are not those who hunger and thirst after righteousness *hallowed* by their perseverance? is it not our own immortal souls that we put at risk in absorbing ourselves in the goods of this world? is Christ no more than *just* that he is the acceptable advocate for our sins?

These words which are so important in the old Bible and so largely disregarded in the new are essentially religious words: they have their natural context within the religious register, which they help to define. Another way of noting the importance of this distinction is to say that the characteristic mode of the Bible is promissory, not informative. This is often explicit in the prophetic books: 'the Lord himself shall give you a sign: Behold, a virgin shall conceive and bear a son and shall call his name Immanuel' (the birth of Jesus is not a confirmation of the *accuracy* of this prophecy, but rather the fulfilment of a promise). In other respects the promissory mode – often identifiable by no more than tone – is more marked in the New Testament. (This allows Paul to be so often hortatory: it is important that he tells his people to rejoice, so that rejoicing becomes something near to a duty.) If we look at the opening of the Sermon on the Mount there may not seem to be much change when we move from the Authorised to the Jerusalem version: even if we admit that 'happy' has not so rich a meaning as 'blessed', the form may look so similar that the loss appears slight:

> Blessed are the poor in spirit: for theirs is the kingdom of heaven.
> Blessed are they that mourn: for they shall be comforted.
> Blessed are the meek: for they shall inherit the earth. Matt. 5:3–5 (AV)

> How happy are the poor in spirit; theirs is the kingdom of heaven.
> Happy the gentle: they shall have the earth for their heritage.
> Happy those who mourn: they shall be comforted. (Jerusalem)

There may even seem to be a welcome eagerness in the ejaculatory opening of the modern set. But actually the change – in intention and meaning – is fundamental. 'Blessed are they that mourn' is grammatically a sentence in the present indicative; but its logic is entirely different from the same sentence with 'happy' replacing 'blessed'. For to say 'Blessed are they that mourn' is not to describe a present state in which those who mourn find themselves; it is to make them a promise, which is identified in the future clause which follows. (The Greek word which the AV renders as 'for' and the Jerusalem leaves out altogether is ὅτι: 'in that' might be an even more explicit reading – blessed are they that mourn in that they will be comforted.) On the other hand, to say 'how happy [are] those who mourn' *is* straightforwardly descriptive of the present, and, when we think about it, decidedly queer, for evidently those who mourn are ipso facto not happy, and even if we understand the clause that follows as explanatory, it cannot explain present happiness as an anticipation of future relief: later comfort may bring later happiness, it cannot cancel the unhappiness of mourning now. But there is no contradiction between mourning and blessedness. Christ's meaning can only be understood if we accept that he is not describing how these people feel or even how they ought to feel, but is offering a sure and certain hope to those who presently mourn. Blessing always contains some kind of gift and has the future within itself: Christ's blessing is his own promise, and *that* is his concern for his people, not how they are feeling at the moment.

At 11:27–8 Luke reports one of those tiny episodes which interrupt the main narrative without immediately apparent purpose yet have power to illuminate all around them. As often it involves someone otherwise unidentified:

> Now as he was speaking, a woman in the crowd raised her voice and said, 'Happy the womb that bore you and the breasts you sucked!' But he replied, 'Still happier those who hear the word of God and keep it!'

That is how the Jerusalem puts it: an obvious ground for quarrelling with this reading is that it doesn't really make sense to speak of a happy womb and breasts, and if this is thought of as an oblique way of talking of Mary's happiness, it is unclear what is gained through the indirection. We might then ask whether the woman in the crowd was talking about happiness at all (why should she do so at such a moment?) – and the doubt is confirmed by Christ's answer. If he is actually describing how it stands with those who keep the word of God, if his sentence is genuinely descriptive, then it must be empirical, and so is always open to be falsified by a single contrary case (there might be someone who keeps the word of God and is nevertheless unhappy). But if what he says is '*Blessed* are they that hear the word of God and keep it', he is not giving information about a certain group of people, not making a statement of any kind, but a promise, as in the Sermon on the Mount he has promised comfort to those that mourn. 'Blessed', therefore, in Christ's mouth, is a performative word, and what he says could only be 'falsified' by non-fulfilment of the promise; but that would not make 'I promise so-and-so' capable of truth or falsity in the way of a descriptive statement. The Jerusalem translators (among others) have made the mistake of approaching the Bible as if it were a book full of *information*, whereas it is not that kind of book at all: it is the word *of* God, not words about God (there is nothing we could say about God by way of description or characterisation, as we describe and characterise objects in the world about us). This misapprehension – a habit of reading all indicative statements as if they are descriptive (historical or scientific) – makes so many apparent generalisations so disturbing, indeed impossible. 'Ask, and it will be given to you; search, and you will find . . . For the one who asks always receives; the one who searches always finds . . . ' (Luke 11:9–10). But *does* the one who asks *always* receive, the one who searches always find? As a general statement this seems obviously untrue. It may not seem to make a great difference to say instead 'everyone that asketh receiveth'; but this form has no trouble-making 'always' (which the Greek will not bear), and second and more importantly, in a context of performative utterances it has the force of a promise that those who ask will not go empty-handed.

The English word 'blessed' behaves in a different way according to the power of the speaker to bless. For it is characteristic that there is the active transitive verb 'to bless', to which 'happy' offers no counterpart. So it is striking and disconcerting that when the Jerusalem translators need a verb they do in fact turn to the old 'bless' – 'bless those who curse you' (Luke 6:28) – which now lacks the essential context of meaning provided by the word's other appearances and must in consequence be very hard to incorporate into one's understanding. The Greek word at this point ($\epsilon \dot{v} \lambda o \gamma \epsilon \hat{\iota} \tau \epsilon$) might seem to invite us to do no more than *speak well* of those who curse us (it is also used in Elizabeth's benediction of Mary: Luke 1:42); but at the blessing at the Last Supper it is again used, though it plainly will not do to think of Christ as *eulogising* the bread. The adjective regularly used is $\mu \alpha \kappa \acute{\alpha} \rho \iota o s$ – traditionally a word used only of the gods as opposed to mortals; the fusing of the two Greek words into the single, profound and complex English one is one of the great discoveries of the old translations – an element in the continuing process of discovering truth within language. To make a related point $\delta \acute{\iota} \kappa \alpha \iota o s$ and $\delta \iota \kappa \alpha \iota o \sigma \acute{v} \nu \eta$ (the words for which the Authorized Version New Testament reserves 'righteous' and 'righteousness') had their origins in conceptions of justice and right which are pre-Christian and in some ways alien to Christianity. But if these conceptions are enough for salvation, Christ had no need to come into the world and teach us what to the Greeks was foolishness. So again it is a matter of forging out of the old materials a new language to create new meanings or make new meanings possible. This is what happened in the first century, and we seem now to be seeing the process in reverse – a retreat from meanings which leaves the words unfamiliar and embarrassing, though the melancholy, long withdrawing roar of the sea of faith is smothered in the relaxing hum of happiness and integrity. The failure of nerve which I suggested above has something much more serious underlying it than mere linguistic awkwardness. The constant intermingling of the two kinds of failure is neatly encapsulated in the Jerusalem's infuriating 'I tell you solemnly' – its substitution for the familiar 'Verily I say unto you' of most of the early versions. Verily the latter phrase is not modern English, but neither is the other: should we not be inclined to laugh at someone who was in the habit of announcing that he was telling us something solemnly? Moreover 'solemnly' runs away from Jesus's intention in using the solemn word 'Amen'

– his point was to insist on the truth, not the solemnity, of what he had to say.

Is it too much to ask translators of the Bible to make statements which are undisguisedly religious, to use the kind of language in which one can talk of God and make palpable our dependence on him? Doubtless these words which I have picked out do sound strange to modern ears: 'righteousness' is hardly current, except when preceded by 'self' (and one thinks of the parallel degeneration of 'pious' and now 'devout' into terms almost of contempt). But the old church knew about this too: the very beautiful and searching Prayer of Humble Access in the Prayer Book Communion service begins, 'We do not presume to come to this thy Table, O merciful Lord, trusting in our own righteousness, but in thy manifold and great mercies:' the allusion is to Ezekiel 33:13, where, as ever, righteousness has given way to integrity: but why should we not trust in our own integrity – as Mr Honest did? Most of us have some notion of whether we are honest or not. If the best that Paul can wish for his church at Philippi is that they be happy, even the 'pagans' do as much, don't they? We are back to the question of the language we use today: in this language the words we need to approach God are missing, because the language (that is, our sensibilities and consciousness) has lost the sense that we need approach him at all. And a word such as righteousness embarrasses us not because it is archaic or refers to some quaint superstition that the modern world has outgrown, but because it can still remind us that there was once a conception of grace beyond natural goodness, or social responsibility, which is what goodness itself has now subsided into. This power of the word may not last much longer as the new Bibles gain ground. The Jerusalem people aimed to make things easier for the modern reader: but to do that they need to eliminate those characteristics of the Bible which make the language recognisable as the word of God, and they have all but succeeded. Making things easier means making them more comfortable: it is easier to agree to the need for integrity than to the need for righteousness, because the latter makes greater demands on us. But if we cannot talk about righteousness, we cannot talk about a right relationship to God; and *if* we cannot, it is because we – all of us who speak the language and keep it alive or let it die – have lost belief in it. What looks like funk in the face of the world's incredulity or derision is worse: it is complicity.

I offer one more example of the kind of reduction which is what the modern translators understand by rendering the text into the language we use today, one that reveals something of what is hidden within the failure of style. Twice when the angel of the apocalypse has pronounced the true sayings of God, Jerusalem's John 'knelt at his feet to worship him, but he said to me, "Don't do that: I am a servant just like you and all your brothers who are witnesses to Jesus. It is God that you must worship." ' (Rev. 19:10) Why will this not do? Obviously something is wrong with the tone (failure of tone is the surest sign of uncertainty or uneasiness of belief): 'Don't do that' suggests either exasperation or a rather ghastly mateyness ('don't be an ass, old chap – I'm only one of you, you know'). The Greek is very terse, but instinct with warning – ὅρα μή – and this comes out unmistakably in the AV's 'See thou do it not': it is a command which John would resist at his peril. The modern angel hints at an impropriety in John's kneeling; the old one warns against the outrage of blasphemy, and his sentence, with its emphatic 'not' kept to the strongest place at the end, enforces this unforgettably. But what could we put in its place? for the sentence is assuredly not in a current idiom. The fact seems to be that we *could not give* a warning in so commanding a way; and I suggest that the reason is that as a people we no longer believe in the authority which would give that kind of command meaning. The evidence of our language is irresistible. Surprising as it may seem at a time when the word 'love' is tossed about with such freedom, we apparently can't say 'Beloved' either, as John does in his epistles, so simply and without coyness. That was his word all right (ἀγαπητοί); but the best we moderns can manage is 'Dear friends' (NEB) or the frightful 'My dear people' (Jerusalem), a stuffy patronising pulpitese which is simply incredible as the language of a real person. But if we cannot say 'Beloved', it can only be because we do not love; and what then becomes of Christ's new commandment?

Be not deceived; God is not mocked (or if you prefer, don't delude yourself into thinking that God can be cheated): for whatsoever a man soweth, that shall he also reap. Robinson noted his impression that the NEB's New Testament 'records a mean, insignificant religious movement'. My own impression after a few years of the Jerusalem is that it was born out of sheer bewilderment. And bewilderment is what readers unaccustomed to solving their problems on the harp will reap. I open the Jerusalem Bible at random and find this:

As it was his purpose to bring a great many of his sons into glory, it was appropriate that God, for whom everything exists and through whom everything exists, should make perfect, through suffering, the leader who would take them to their salvation. For

the one who sanctifies, and the ones who are sanctified, are of the
same stock; that is why he openly calls them brothers.

(Heb. 2:10–11)

What on earth – or in heaven – is this about? It seems past analysing;
and anyone who thinks he is seized of the 'argument' which the
form appears to profess is almost certainly fooling himself. The God
whose name turns up so inexplicably cannot be the one whom Paul
and John the Divine worshipped, for this one undoubtedly is
mocked by the paraphernalia which surrounds him. The true God
is nowhere near, for who is he that he should have his actions
deemed 'appropriate' by men? The notion reminds one of the weird
imitation-Jesus who asks in the NEB 'What is your opinion about
the Messiah?' Answer: it is one of Handel's best oratorios. As if
Christ needed our *opinion* of the Messiah: who are we to have
opinions about the Messiah? The NEB in this passage from Hebrews
is even more impertinent, talking indeed of what was 'clearly fitting'
for God. Does it need saying that to be impertinent about God is
impious?

Paradoxically the seeming simplicity and directness of the opening
of Genesis shows the same attempt to reduce God to the language
of commonsense and so to the measure of *l'homme moyen sensuel*.
'There was darkness over the deep, and God's spirit hovered over
the water.' Why should it do that? The word has the wrong kind
of precision, for hovering is what kestrels and helicopters do, and
the ludicrous impression is given that God might be trying to peer
through the darkness to see what was in the water; so the creation
of light which follows has the air of a pantomime trick. Compare:
'darkness was upon the face of the deep: and the Spirit of God
moved upon the face of the waters.' I do not know whether this is
a more or less 'accurate' translation than the other; and I know that
I cannot understand it with my merely rational mind, for there is
in the language itself that which shares in the unfathomable mystery
of creation. In that way it must take us closer to God's act and to
his word, to speak which we must have a language in which his
name is at home: only then can we hope to find him through and
in it. The constancy with which this is so in the Authorised Version
is the measure of its greatness. In the modern versions by contrast,
it seems to have been necessary to go on inventing new gods to fit
the narrow space which is all that is available within such religious
conceptions as we can achieve. To translate the Bible worthily it is
not enough to be moved by a desire to deepen theological thought
or keep abreast with the times: one must need to speak the word of
God – for which we need a language of God: in order to believe we
need a language in which the act of belief is possible.

When you speak with so great a Lord, it is well that you should think of Who it is that you are addressing, and what you yourself are, if only that you may speak to him with proper respect.

ST TERESA OF AVILA
The Way of Perfection

A *poesis* of recurrence
J. P. WARD

'When iron, cast into the fire, loses its rust, and becomes all bright with burning, so the man that turneth himself wholly to God is divested of all sloth, and changeth into a new man.' That is from Thomas à Kempis's *The Imitation of Christ*. The simile is lucid and approachable. But what we also feel, and cannot avoid, is the *intention* of the writer; he *wants* us to think of a changed man in this way. That is hardly surprising, for intentionality is a common characteristic of all language other than specialised language or metalanguage. Language directs our attention away from itself, not only to the thing to which it refers but also to the motive or energy behind the language itself. The words do not simply lie flat on the page or sound on the waves of air. They are directed there.

I introduce these points about language because I have recently tried to examine what could be meant by 'religious language', and particularly the Bible. For several decades the Bible has been subjected to immense microscopic and scientific research. The words on the page have been taken and examined for what light we can throw on their date of origin, their authorship as measured by linguistic, stylistic and other counts, how their factual content compares with contemporary but non-religious records, and how the same information fits with what we know from archaeological, numismatic, anthropological and other sources. Thus we can now state confidently that the book of Isaiah is by at least three different authors, that Mark is the earliest gospel and that Phil. 2:6 ('thought it not robbery to be equal with God. . .') is probably from an already existing poem.[1] It is a great gain to have this mass of information; and the sense of clarity, lucidity and burden-lifting freedom with which we can now read the Bible contrasts with that surely stifling constraint the experience must often have been for earlier generations to whom the Bible was in some sense 'infallible'. Indeed the detached attitude now taken to the central book of our culture by all its serious scholars is in one sense the greatest logical act of faith in its importance.

Yet such investigations, being broadly or narrowly scientific, are by that fact conducted at a certain fixed level of focus of attention. From their point of view the text has to be regarded as just that:

'documents' and 'texts', and objectively. But the Bible as phenomenon at other levels remains; indeed, it is enhanced. If it is now
'fallible' then what is our undeniable heritage of a sense of the
memorability of its words; what is that phenomenon? In what sense,
if any, is it a religious work, consisting of religious language (that
is, not just language about God, but language directed to God, or
considered to be coming from God); what becomes of such claims?
In the hermeneutic terms with which I began, what is the motive
or drive behind the language? If it is not infallible, in what sense is
it a book of ultimate concern, and what in its language makes us
feel that to be so?

I recently read the King James version of the Bible. I should say
here that I am no biblical scholar or theologian of any sort. It was
in reading of the Midianites and the Amalekites in Judges 7 that I
felt that a central motif, hitherto noticed sporadically, was asserting
a greater dominance, in resonance and structural depth, than anything else. 'And their camels were without number, as the sand by
the sea side for multitude' (v. 20). That image had been used at
least four times already; it is in Genesis twice (22:17 and 32:12),
where God promises Abraham and Jacob severally that he will
multiply their descendants; it numbers the grains of corn Joseph
collected (Gen. 41:9); the Philistines; the Israelites; Judah and
Israel; and even God's thoughts (1 Sam. 13:5; 2 Sam. 17:11; 1
Kings 4:20; Psalm 139:18, respectively). But it was not the image,
but its recurrence, that was beginning to seem important. Doubtless
later writers copied earlier ones. In a different way, other types of
recurrence had been used in different contexts. In the story of
Samson's betrayal by Delilah (Judges 16) one of the Bible's many
threefold repetitions occurs. Each time Samson affects to tell Delilah
of the source of his strength she, having removed that source, uses
a trick to test whether his strength has gone: 'The Philistines be
upon thee Samson.' That is, the three-part structure of the story
has a surface projection in that saying. Samuel, of course, is called
by God three times (1 Sam. 3). These examples are no doubt expli-
cable enough. It dawns on the reader, however, that these cases fit
into a wider pattern of recurrence altogether. We meet it in the first
chapter of the entire Bible in a very formal and stately movement:
'And the evening and the morning were the fourth day . . . And
the evening and the morning were the fifth day.' An exact formal
repetition is built into the very way the story is told. We then
experience a succession of stories from the expulsion from the garden of Eden through to the establishment of the covenant by God
to Moses at Mount Sinai. There is Abraham and Isaac's sacrifice;

Jacob and Esau and the pottage; Jacob and Laban's daughters; all
the Joseph stories; the plagues, Passover, and Exodus; and many
more. Repetition is apparent enough in the stories of the plagues,
but two other kinds of recurring motif strike us. The stories seem
to proceed across a flat, levelled plain of imaginative scope; they
follow each other in linear fashion and seem to carry equal weight.
They do not swell into a climax, except in the sense that each one
is itself a climax. (The real climax is the establishment of the Law
itself.) And the entire generational story is a sequence of statements,
events and actions, not interwoven in a complex hierarchy or organ-
ism but progressively connected by hundreds and hundreds of 'ands'
– as many, we might say, as is the sand by the sea side for multitude.
One can open the early books almost anywhere to check the effect
of this. We are constrained to accept the stories as examples within
a succession of recurrences. But when we come to the Law and the
covenant, recurrence comes up in a new way altogether. The syntactical repetition there provides a coverage by which every aspect
of life can be accounted for legally. 'If a man sell his daughter . . .
If a man smite the eye of his servant . . . If an ox gore a man. . .'
The tenfold initial commandments (Exodus 20:1–17) are the first
statement in a series of static, unalterable directives for all conceivable circumstances, from the design of the tabernacle to the exact
detail of procedure in the five Offerings, and the right understanding
of the clean and unclean. There are the religious, civil and criminal
statutes. This is the weight of the last three books of the Pentateuch;
Leviticus, Numbers and Deuteronomy. But there is also a census
of the people (Num. 26 and 27); that is, the deep structure of this
repetitive syntax is found just as much where dead fact rather than
injunction is the nature of the message.

So what we have, then, is writing in which patterns are repeated,
no matter what the subject to which the pattern refers, and indeed
no matter what the pattern itself is. We have a recurrence motif,
dealing with not this or that but with *recurrence itself*. Linguistically,
structural occurrences of repetition appear as a fundamental matter,
more fundamental and underlying than the diversity of the material
which they transport. I suggest that this dominates the Bible, not
merely in the obvious cases like the parallelism of the Psalms or the
four-part repetition of the gospel story, but even in Paul and the
Epistles too. It is different there, differently done, but that would
underline the point all the more, that however different the context,
motivation, or authorial personality, the recurrence theme is not
avoided.

Many things might be said about this motif. Some would say it is simply the familiar matter of primitive expression in civilisation prior to the huge freedoms expressed in (for example) Elizabethan language and Shakespeare, or the equally large modernist convolutions found in the nineteenth-century novel and modern literature itself. The short answers to this, in the space available, are, first, that it is quite different in Homer, where the degree of uniform illumination of everyday detail, foregrounding of every present event, and a most unhurried and leisurely procedure of activity,[2] wholly disperse any oppressively historical or temporal progress in which 'recurrence' itself in all its forms is deployed as a set of markers. But in any case, even if these characteristics are indeed found more in earlier civilisations than now, that does not tell us what they are doing there. A reading of the whole Bible (not just the parts my description has reached so far) suggests all kinds of underlying drive, intention and compulsion behind the phenomenon I have called recurrence. In some places it is oppressive, and in uniform syntactical arrangement the Law lies heavily upon us; there are no chinks or gaps, changes of mind, self-analyses, ideogrammatic writing (*à la* Pound) or stream-of-consciousness. The oppression comes from outside. At other times it is compulsive rather than oppressive; or even impulsive: 'Praise the Lord with the harp/Sing unto him with the psaltery and an instrument of ten strings/ Sing unto him a new song/Play skilfully with a loud noise. . .' (Psalm 33). In the Epistles it is usually a compulsion to diversify homogeneously every possible component on a given theme ('. . . whatsoever things are true, whatsoever things are honest, whatsoever things are just, whatsoever things are pure. . .') and the homogeneity again appears as recurrence. Recurrence itself is what seems dominant, not the recurrence of one or another main theme, although, of course, those recur and recur too.

There are other possible explanations of biblical recurrence. It may be argued, with Leach[3], that this is 'redundancy'; the idea in communications theory that repetition basically reinforces communication. But this biblical recurrence is not merely plurality. In the Book of Proverbs, for example, there is certainly considerable reinforcement, so that on some occasions there are exact repetitions ('It is better to dwell in a corner of the housetop/Than with a brawling woman in a wide house' – both 21:9 and 25:24), and in other places it appears both in the two hemistiches of a verse and also over successive verses; for example, 'Answer a fool according to his folly/Lest he be wise in his own conceit./He that sendeth a message by the hand of a fool/Cutteth off the feet, and drinketh damage.' (26:5–6) But the total impression of the Proverbs is not simply of reinforcement as an instrumental device. The book's inorganic structure leaves its proverbs and maxims in tension with one another. They are thus not simply a series of directives but a basis for thought, for consideration; in fact, for wisdom. We thus have the impression of the author himself as deeply speculative, and engaging in speculation at the moment of writing. The wisdom atmosphere, so to speak, is what is achieved by the succession of more or less (though not always) inorganically related postulates. This may well not be conscious on the writer's part, but it is still in the broader sense intentional, because the drive from behind, the pressure that forces the words into existence and into their place, is of a certain kind, and can be read from the language. Different kinds of pattern of recurrence point to different drive-forces behind themselves. We have said already that it is oppressive in one context, compulsive in another, impulsive and even exuberant in another, and now speculative in Proverbs. In the New Testament, as I hope to argue, it is different again. Redundancy does not seem the main point.

It might equally be argued that 'recurrence' comes from the event of many hands in one book, and is therefore stylistic. If one analyses any writer at all one finds *some* predominant motifs, otherwise that writer would have no identity. Therefore when there is a collection of writers one might say that we have recurrence recurring. The point is important, because biblical scholars have devoted considerable energy to stylistic analysis of biblical writers (showing for example that Jeremiah is not by one man, nor are the Psalms, and so on.) But again this does not refute our contention. Reading the Bible at the receptive-interpretative level suggested shows more than merely a recurrence of motifs. The writers seem to be in the *grip* of the form of recurrence, and it thus becomes very explicit. It is as though what they have to say *demands* to be encased in this very exact, haunting patterning, no matter how different such patterning is from one writer to another. There are, of course, any amount of exceptions to this motif, what we might call 'individual' or unique writing in a different sense (as in the more Blakean, manic parts of Isaiah; e.g., 6:1 ff; 8:1.ff; 21:11, and certain other insulated items I will refer to later); but the hemistiches of the Psalms, the tripartite approach of Delilah and to Samuel – and to Peter, when he denies – the seven-part first chapter of Genesis, the 'Woe unto you', 'Thus saith the Lord', and other refrains, are not merely style in general but a very firm, insistent, repeated *kind* of style which seems to have a profoundly linguistic, not just temporal-historical or political-legal, origin.

Before drawing inferences let us continue with a few further examples of how recurrence stretches on through the rest of the Old Testament and into the New. In Joshua and Judges the relentless, often violent carrying out of the purpose of the Lord comes in language we would technically call monotonous; kings are listed and the division of the land detailed. In Ruth, the pivotal passage shows how devotion and love, in their turn, are expressed by linguistic recurrence which is this time binary: 'Whither thou goest, I will go; and where thou lodgest, I will lodge; thy people shall be my people, and thy God my God: where thou diest, will I die, and there will I be buried. . .' In 1 Kings 8 we find Solomon's prayer, and it is extended in 2 Chr. 6. The prayer is both prayerful and legalistic. Every eventuality is covered ('If there be dearth in the land . . . If thy people go out to war against their enemies . . . If they sin against thee . . .'), so that when we pray, 'Hear thou in heaven thy dwelling-place, and when thou hearest, forgive.' Recurrence is a most beautiful hum and resonance in this prayer, but to a quite different end from that of Delilah or Ruth or the writer of Genesis 1. The Book of Job is extraordinary. Here the recurrence is compulsive. It is as though, prior to what the modern world calls enlightenment perhaps, Job and his answers must say everything as many times as possible, to make it true, or to make themselves feel it true. This is as much where Job is reviling himself as when he is acceding, finally, to God, or when his companions answer on God's behalf. All of nature, it seems, is cited as evidence (the references to nature are a recurrence, for quite different purpose, in the Psalms and Isaiah), but a new kind of recurrence is the proliferation of rhetorical questions. Chapters 6, 38 and 41 are almost wholly of that kind, and rhetorical questions are dispersed elsewhere also. Thus recurrence again serves a new purpose, this time to find a road out of anguish.

It is difficult to do justice to the evidence in a paper of this scope. The Psalm's parallelism is perhaps a matter sufficiently formal not to need further argument. Isaiah, it seems, *is* a more individual visionary (the three main parts are by at least three authors but they share a prophetic tradition[4]), yet the 'Woe unto you' theme dominates (chapters 5, 10, 18, 28 and elsewhere); and also in Isaiah (the first Isaiah) there is a motif of incantation, the raised voice, the ejaculation or cry: 'Woe unto you . . .!' itself, 'How art thou fallen from heaven O Lucifer!' 'Howl, ye ships of Tarshish!' 'Give ye ear, and hear my voice, hearken. . .', which, like other themes, would need more examination than is here possible. In Ezekiel the exact refrain is 'The word of the Lord came unto me again, saying. . .', and this recurs over a dozen times. In the minor prophets, in Joel, Nahum and elsewhere, the recurrence of one theme overhangs everything – the Lord; the Lord saith; the iniquity of Israel; the judgment upon nations, the desolation of Egypt, until the end, and the last sentence of the Old Testament, 'lest I come and smite the earth with a curse,' leaving us with a sense of the Old Testament's unconsummated conclusion.

There has been much argument about the connection between the two testaments, and even the desirability or otherwise of retaining the Old Testament as part of the canon.[5] From the New Testament I will refer to the gospels, the epistles as a unit, and (briefly) Revelation. On reading, it seemed to me that while on the one hand the New Testament, and the gospels particularly, give a quite new sense of liberation from the oppressiveness of Old Testament 'recurrence', nevertheless the New Testament, in a very different way, uses recurrence motifs just as dominantly and explicitly. Clearly, it is crucial to establish this, if it be true, because any idea that the Bible's real or imagined identity as the 'Word of God' is coexistent with the nature of its language, depends on the consistency of this theme in the New Testament as well, and the centrality of the gospels to it also.

As already said, the New Testament immediately carries on the recurrence motif, if at a different dimension altogether, in that the gospels themselves are four occurrences of one story or event. I can only say that my own experience, after traversing the Old Testament books with considerable effort, was one almost of modernity in the gospels. This shadowy figure who is at the heart of them, yet who seems very immediate indeed (so that we see an old woman 'touch the hem of his garment' – very tentatively it seems; and who stops under a tree, looks up and sees a man hiding there) seems to embody a wholly new freedom and existentiality. It is of course partly because so much more space is given to the figure of Jesus than any other biblical character. But equally 'The Lord' of the Old Testament, who 'saith' and smiteth and punisheth, and so on, is simply not there. For both these reasons it must be that the recurrence motif is of a different order. It seems in the synoptic gospels that very evident recurrences are themselves responsible for precisely this freedom. After the story of the birth (in Matthew and Luke) and before the story of the crucifixion and resurrection in all three, we have simply a series of encapsulated narratives of, basically, three kinds; parables, miracles and confrontations. It is of course considerably different in John, and we come now to that gospel. The encapsulations seem to be separate bubbles of vivid teaching, incident or graphic description. Each piece is a small, self-contained matter; it comes from nowhere, begins, ends and is gone. The encapsulations, then, are the new motif of recurrence, serving as a series of containers for all each writer can remember. Time and again a section begins 'And when Jesus was come up from. . .' and ends '. . . But he departed out of the midst of them. . .' or similarly. Again the underlying 'and' pattern is a ground-beat of recurrence as in much of the Old Testament ('. . . and the rain descended, and the floods came, and the winds blew, and beat upon that house; and it fell; and great was the fall of it.'[6]) Something similar is found in Malory for example, but the Bible's constraining pressure is stronger. But equally to the point are these isolated encapsulations or 'bubbles' to which we have referred. 'And when Jesus was entered into Capernaum', 'And when he was entered into a ship' – and we know that another small story is under way. All of this is familiar enough, and has been commented on. But it is this isolation – resulting from a *recurrence* of encapsulations – that liberates. The miracles, for example, do not amount to a system. Jesus just does turn water into wine, then cure a man let down through a roof, then raise someone from the dead, then transfer a catatonic mania into some pigs, then walk on the water of the sea, and so forth. In the parables the repetition is more explicit in that many refer to themselves as a variation on the one before in terms of the object illustrated: 'Again, the kingdom of heaven is like unto . . .' The very immediacy and domesticity of these parables, often noted, as well as the immediacy of the miraculous incidents, as it were capitalises on their insulation to stand out all the more clearly, like some newly-picked fruit, or newly-made and polished chair or table. The third set of encapsulations is the confrontations. Again there is a recurring hum or resonance which we recognise as soon as we come to it. There is the introduction, such as 'Then went the Pharisees, and took counsel how they might entangle him in his talk' (Matt. 22:15); there is the story, Jesus' answer, and the close.

Of course I have made the picture over-simple,[7] but I think the other features of the synoptic gospels hang round this one. In John we seem to have a swaying movement, gently back and forward, between those who accuse Jesus, and himself and his answers. If John, even more than the other gospel writers, gives us theology rather than narrative (as is now thought by most scholars) then all the more can Jesus' accusers in the confrontations be thought of as *advocati diaboli* in John's mind, even though he knew, presumably, to what extent this ascription was also historically justified. But in another sense too, in John, recurrence does move in a different direction from that of the synoptic gospels. Here John is walking round his thoughts; very direct but thought-out claims stem from immediate incident (whether in event or parable) leading to intellectual, metaphysical and devotional speculation. Recurrence, as explicit as ever, moves inward to the passages themselves. The opening passage of the gospel is too famous to need quoting, nor does it need arguing that the chief concepts of beginning, word, light, God, world, interweave and play round each other while retaining, however, their undiluted exactitude, their unqualified consistency, as the concepts they begin and end in being. It is the same with the story of the woman of Samaria at the well, where 'water', 'drink' and 'life' do a kind of grave and formal dance with each other, and do not have their power added to or lessened in any occasion of their use. Exactly the same occurs in the section on the Good Shepherd. 'I am the good shepherd: the good shepherd giveth his life for the sheep. But he that is an hireling, and not the shepherd, whose own the sheep are not, seeth the wolf coming, and leaveth the sheep, and fleeth. . .' It is like a set of firm, clear fingerprints. At a later stage in the argument I want to refer to the way the gospel ends.

There are some recurrence themes in the Acts of the Apostles, though not many,[8] and we must now consider the epistles. I will take the supposedly Pauline ones as a whole, aware that the Epistle to the Ephesians, for example, is now not thought to be by Paul, a fact which makes my reading of it, to me at least, the more surprising. Taking a bird's eye view of the texture of Paul's (we will call him that) writing, we sense not a walking-around, as with John, but a great opening-out, as though every avenue must be looked down and every point followed. In the Epistle to the Romans the little marker 'What then? . . .' 'What shall we say then?' recurs, as new possibilities or difficulties arise. Paul's wrestlings in his own mind feel parallel to those of Socrates in the Greek tradition: for the first time they have a dialectical quality. But we then come quickly to this passage: '. . . being filled with all unrighteousness, fornication, wickedness, covetousness, maliciousness; full of envy, murder, debate, deceit, malignity; whisperers, backbiters, haters of God, despiteful, proud, boasters, inventors of evil things, disobedient to parents, without understanding, covenantbreakers, without natural affection, implacable, unmerciful. . .' (Romans 1:29–31). This is very Pauline. It is not the wish to rub it in, but the wish to cover everything, and mention every possibility or member of the catalogue. Here is 1 Cor. 12

. . . to one is given by the Spirit the word of wisdom; to another the word of knowledge by the same Spirit; to another faith by the same Spirit; to another the gifts of healing by the same Spirit; to another the working of miracles; to another prophecy; to another discerning of spirits; to another divers kinds of tongues; to another the interpretation of tongues; but all these worketh that one and the selfsame Spirit, dividing to every man severally as he will.

Other examples of this characteristic are the universally-known subsequent chapter in which charity, too, is broken down into its component parts; Romans 12:6–18, with its twenty-nine injunctions for Christian living; 2 Cor. 7 (details of how to be Christ's ambassador); the famous 'whatsoever things are true. . .' (Phil. 4:8), already quoted; and, most explicit perhaps, the extended metaphor of 'the whole armour of God' (Eph. 6:11), in which shoes, shield, breastplate, helmet and other parts are given their various spiritual functions. In the light of these passages, which seem to stand out so clearly from the surrounding searches, qualifications, questionings, probes and analyses, we can understand the summary phrases of Paul like 'let all things be done decently and in order' (1 Cor. 11:40), and '. . . Christ, from whom the whole body fitly joined together. . .' which seem to suggest the writer's ideal, and his compulsion; and, most of all, the idea (troublesome to some) of being 'all things to all men', which on the tendency I am pointing to here merely suggests that all things have their rightful place. It is as though every possible aspect of anything must be referred to. But again, the drift of these quotations is the way their parts all seem equal and equally weighted examples of the matter in question at the time; again then they are recurrences. Again differing from the Old Testament and now from the gospels too, it seems that biblical writing, as here illustrated, has to centre round this strain toward an emerging, re-emerging, and re-emerging again, example of the same thing, idea, obsession, law, hemistich, type of incident, injunction, or any other thing, being *done again*, so that it seems to stand in sequence to the cases of itself which preceded it.

In Revelation there is the exact marching appearance of the 'seven churches', attended to in equal balance one by one, and exactly recalling to us, fortuitously perhaps, the first chapter of Genesis. Revelation was not the last book to be written[9], but has been canonised as last. The end of John's gospel came across in my reading as the pivot of the entire scriptural canon. Everything in the Bible after it, feels like outcome. The end (bar two verses) is this:

> 'Jesus saith unto him, If I will that he tarry till I come, what is that to thee? Follow thou me. Then went this saying abroad among the brethren, that that disciple should not die: yet Jesus said not unto him, He shall not die; but, if I will that he tarry till I come, what is that to thee?' (John 21:22–3).

That extremely deliberate piece of recurrence, right at the end of the last, most thoughtful and elaborated version of the life of Jesus, seems to draw our attention to recurrence itself. It says that words were said and that it is saying them again. It seems possible that this 'recurrence' is what people have experienced as a result of which they say that the Bible is God's Word, or that God's Holy Spirit moves through the Bible and indeed generates it. It functions at a sufficiently deep structural level to constrain the biblical writers no matter what their differences in history or in personality. It seems also that this motif is behind (though not synonymous with) the qualities of the Bible which make people call it inspired, or indeed poetic. We need to consider these points, particularly because of new translations of the Bible, although I am in no position to analyse these translations in detail.

In saying recurrence is behind the idea of the Bible as God's Word, I mean not simply recurrence's mathematical patterns, but that as intended (as we said at the start) or forced through from behind, from some source or sources such that, when subjected to the constraints of recurrence, it has seemed like a single, massive, energising thrust, or commanding power. We can either indeed believe that this is God's Spirit, or that the compulsions, obsessions, motives and anxieties of so many people, subjected to the one motif, can have that spiritual effect when a whole literature is transfused; in this case that of the ancient Hebrews and then the Christian world. It is exceedingly important, for it seems to put the language of the Bible ahead of the history in the Bible; it seems to imply that our understanding of this history comes from what is, after all, perhaps the unique quality of human beings; namely, language. And this constraining of history by language in the Bible has been most interestingly illustrated precisely by the most recent scholarly discoveries about the gospels; the point that the historical Jesus does indeed elude us, not because we happen to lack sufficient evidence in the gospels of his life but because the gospels do not try to capture historical events literally; they are not that kind of writing.[10]

But this universal recurrent restraint is also experienced as inspired, as 'the beautiful words of the Bible', and as poetic. If this occurs without any explicit intention of the writers to write poems (with the assumptions and conventions associated with poetry) then it needs explaining. We can do this by distinguishing two main kinds of poetry, and also making another kind of distinction – not the same one, although they overlap – between poetry in general and sacred writing. For the language of the Bible, although often inspired and throughout bearing the stamp of a certain *poesis*, is not of itself poetry. But let us first consider a well-known passage of Shakespeare:

> To-morrow, and to-morrow, and to-morrow,
> Creeps in this petty pace from day to day,
> To the last syllable of recorded time;
> And all our yesterdays have lighted fools
> The way to dusty death. Out, out, brief candle!
> Life's but a walking shadow; a poor player,
> That struts and frets his hour upon the stage,
> And then is heard no more; it is a tale
> Told by an idiot, full of sound and fury,
> Signifying nothing.
>
> *Macbeth, V.v.*

Here the recurrence does *not* seem to dominate. Where that appears at all it helps the passage to spread out rather than constrain it into one's motif subservience. Each line produces a *new* kind of vowel-sound and emphasis, and image, even if on occasion connections with a previous one are present. We have the imagery of steps and pace, changing to the verbal idea 'syllable', then the idea of fools and idiots; candle-light; dust; the stage; great noise; these all in a deeply unfolding, rather than recurrent, structure. The poet furthermore urges the words themselves, according to their separate powers of association, to expend energy on getting the intention across. We may consider how the words 'creeps . . . petty . . . pace. . .' seem to make us stop on them and emphasise *them*, quite unlike the separate words in 'and the evening and the morning were the fifth day', where recurrence, both internally (evening, . . . morning) and externally to other verses (fifth – fourth – third) is all. It is the same in twentieth-century imagist poetry and that of its descendants, those declared devotees of the 'word-hoard', such as Basil Bunting and David Jones. The emphasis in their work is on what can be released from the words themselves.

Writing considered to be sacred does not seem like that. Its poetic effects, when they occur, have a different origin. In these it is the writing's structure rather than its mined verbal resources, its rich vocabulary, that is important. There is of course a kind of poetry which is like this – for example, Clare's 'I am; yet what I am, none cares nor knows', and much of Donne's love poetry, and Edward Thomas and Hardy – which is why we were able to say that there is a distinction between two kinds of poetry as well as one between poetry and sacred writing. (Milton clearly uses both kinds of poetry with great power in *Paradise Lost*). But with sacred writing, we are suggesting that not only the recurrence motif but its envisaged origin in the power and purpose of God are what are important. The sacred writer (and we are not talking about strictly religious poetry like the Psalms or Herbert or Hopkins, which is a special matter) is not motivated by the need to write poems. His aim is to be a channel for the will of God, God's Spirit and God's Word. He dare not stray too far from it, for it is the *one* God whose spirit commands. And for precisely this reason there is in this writing the most fundamental structure of recurrences, for 'recurrence' enables the embodiment of unity without being merely limiting, limiting in a mechanical sense. It is conceived of as the unity of, in effect, an almighty power.

Therefore, when poetic power and effects occur in sacred writing, they would be expected to do so in that context. Here are some examples of what I mean, and not all of them at first sight may seem poetry at all. Their effect however is powerful, and I would say poetic. Here is the story of Abimelech in the battle of Thebez.

> And a certain woman cast a piece of a millstone upon Abimelech's head, and all to break his skull. Then he called hastily unto the young man his armourbearer, and said unto him, Draw thy sword, and slay me, that men say not of me, A woman slew him. And his young man thrust him through, and he died. (Judges 9:53–5).

A clearly profiled value, that of not being shamed by death at the hand of a woman, is merged inseparably with the fewest, sharpest details to create a separable unit, a small cameo, which is wholly convincing, and seemingly projected outward from its surroundings. Again, in the story of Samson, there is the incident where foxes' tails have torches tied to them and they are sent through the enemies' corn to burn it. A quite different example is the universally-known passage where Job seems suddenly to identify, as we would now say, what is most important to him in his suffering, and what he most lacks. 'But where shall wisdom be found?/And where is the place of understanding?/Man knoweth not the price thereof/Neither is it found in the land of the living/The deep saith, it is not in me,/ and the sea saith, it is not with me.' I will give one more example, because the matter seems to be important enough to deserve emphasis. At the end of John's gospel Mary is at the tomb, sees it is empty, sees Jesus, and thinks he is the gardener. But he speaks. 'Jesus saith unto her, Mary. She turned herself, and saith unto him, Rabboni; which is to say, Master.' The recognition's completeness is effected by the absence of adverb; we are *not* told that Jesus spoke firmly, knowingly, graciously or lovingly, nor that Mary's response was joyous, incredulous or fervent. Those realities are conveyed without the words at all; again, they emerge from the surrounding context, and the incident seems to come clean away.

These 'found poems', as we may call them, differ from that poetry which expresses *by* words an embryonically felt conception. Rather, these effects emerge from the context, and from the constraining pressure that holds that context in its linear and historical progression. These incidents and small completenesses seem ejected from that, as we press an orange pip from our fingers by pressure. They may thus be called poetic, for by a few words they combine economy with vivid presence, as poems do, but, unlike poems, that occurs from the pressure of other surrounding writing; in short, from the recurrence motif, which at near or far distance controls the writing at all points.

And what is the implication? Well, when in the New English Bible Jesus says 'Come and have breakfast' (John 21:12) I sense the sacred pressure is missing, although my example is taken out of context too. I think the NEB translators decided to resist any temptation to 'fine writing' in a pejorative sense, or what I suggested was the richly verbal, Shakespearean way, as argued above. In this they were no doubt right. But in so doing, they left themselves stranded as secular men in a secular century, for they seemingly did not open themselves to any inner pressure, any drive from behind, corresponding to what in biblical language is synonymous with recurrence. We might unkindly say, as some have[11], that this is because they are no longer believers; alternatively that they were like the theologians who have studied the Bible from a perspective of science and scholarly detachment. If the second is true, the aim has been to produce a translation at all points accurate and comprehensible in contemporary terms. But if the perspective is always one of detachment and accuracy, and the finding of a correct and precise *individual* word or expression, then the drive from behind and the constraint to recurrence are lost. The result is necessarily limpness, and no inspiration, for there is nothing to force that into existence. A few brief examples may show this. We have mentioned the Jesus-Mary scene; it is the same when Jesus meets Thomas. Thomas simply says, my Lord, and my God. The translators add a wholly superfluous exclamation mark! The effect is instantly a little strident, even hysterical. Because the translators do not feel, continuously and permanently, the recurrent pressure from behind, they have to add it externally by punctuation. Then there is Jesus' prayer in John's gospel; 'Father, the hour is come; glorify thy son . . .', a passage very similar in its modes of recurrence to those of the woman of Samaria and the Good Shepherd, already quoted; a passage which for union of resonance, theology and authority is perhaps unequalled in the Bible. Here the translators simply lose their nerve. They retain 'thee' and 'thou', 'hadst' and 'didst', and anachronistic phrases like 'sovereign over all mankind'. Again the translators simply do not feel in their own contemporary language the thrust necessarily to take on the passage at all. The final example illustrates more explicitly the point about recurrence. 'And he saith unto me, Write, Blessed are they which are called unto the marriage supper of the Lamb. And he saith unto me, These are the true sayings of God.' (Rev. 19:9). For the second 'saith' the NEB has 'added' – 'and he added, These are. . . .' *Added* indeed! shouts Ian Robinson, now with total exasperation.[12] The tension of the passage is wholly lost, for the resonance of the repeated word is gone, as a result of what sounds like mistrust.

Karl Barth, in a theology which many certainly find far too traditional, but which is nonetheless impressive for its profound understanding of the place of religious language in religious life, and for his willingness to accord the Bible the autonomy of power it seems (from whatever source) to have, says that the authority for calling the Bible God's Word is that it just does so impose itself on each occasion; that event keeps occurring[13]. Dogmatic as that may sound, Barth at least takes the invigorating risk of facing that no *other* proof or guarantee of that status is available to us. As generations evolve and develop, new translations will and must occur; that to some extent is the Bible's life. Such translations can only occur from the pressure described, and the way is a poesis of recurrence.

References

1 R. P. Martin, *Carmen Christi: Philippians 2:5–11*, Cambridge University Press, 1967, cited in *Biblical Criticism*, R. Davidson and A. R. C. Leaney, Pelican, 1970.

2 The phrases are all Erich Auerbach's (*Mimesis: the representation of reality in western literature*, trs. Willard R. Trask, Princeton University Press, 1953, chapter 1.)

3 Edmund Leach, *Genesis as Myth*, Cape, 1969, p 8 ff.

4 For an extended discussion cf. G. W. Anderson, *A Critical Introduction to the Old Testament*, Duckworth, 1959, pp 106–20.

5 Most influentially Rudolf C. Bultmann, 'Prophecy and Fulfilment', in *Essays*, 1949 (cited in Davidson and Leaney); also Anderson, op. cit., and C. H. Dodd, *The Authority of the Bible*, Collins, 1960 (first published 1929), esp. chapter 8.

6 The entire Sermon on the Mount, of course, is structured recurrently like the more numerical structurings of the OT, with the nine parallel Beatitudes and then the explicit introduction to each following injunction: 'Ye have heard that it was said in old time. . . .' Matt. 5–7.

7 In Luke there is a further pattern of chiasmus and paradox, thus: 'The first shall be last and the last first'; 'To him that hath shall be given, but from him that hath not shall be taken even that which he hath' – which would take much more analysis.

8 It has been described, together with Esther, Ruth and Daniel, as a 'novel'. So for that matter have *Troilus and Crysede* and *Pilgrim's Progress:* not, to my mind, to much purpose.

9 Davidson and Leaney, pp 326–8.

10 Intriguingly argued in Paul M. Van Buren, *The Secular Meaning of the Gospel, based on analysis of its language*, SCM Press, 1963 – but many less radical than Van Buren would agree.

11 Cf. Ian Robinson, 'Religious English', *Cambridge Quarterly*, II, 4, 1967, pp 303–38.

12 Robinson, p 317.

13 Karl Barth, *Church Dogmatics*, I, part 1, T. & T. Clark, Edinburgh, 1936, chapter 4, section 2, especially p 120.

The Christian God of both church and chapel is approached by worship which is low-toned, pragmatic and unemotional. Where the Anglicans are concerned, the national attitude towards religion, seemly, decorous, polite, restrained, sensible, still dominates both the personal and the intellectual. Suffolk farm-workers use the incomparable English of the Book of Common Prayer and the King James Bible with naturalness and ease. Modern translations and the 1967 new Communion Service do not possess for them the virtue of the immense Elizabethan and Stuart incantations. Simplification is bafflement.

RONALD BLYTHE
Akenfield: portrait of an English village

Texts and contexts
FRASER STEEL

A latecomer to the feast, I spent my first eighteen years in almost complete ignorance of the contents of the Book of Common Prayer. Brought up an English Presbyterian, I had little occasion to know of it. Of course, it was an inevitable item on the educational agenda: A-level history gave me an easy familiarity with its theological niceties before I came by more than an inkling of the character of its prose. That happened at Cambridge – a good place, since Simeon's day, for sudden conversions; but this was no blinding light. Simply, through the college chapel, I was exposed to Evensong, and gradually won to an appreciation of its authority, its sonorous tranquillity, its good order and its grace. For the first time it occurred to me that the act of public worship could be in itself a pleasure – 'our duty and our joy', in one of the few felicities of Series 3. It seemed a natural expansion from the Presbyterian tradition of worship into a richer common memory and a more spacious order. The transition was eased, indeed, by the presence of that common possession of the reformed churches, the Authorised Version of the Bible; but, beyond that, the Anglican liturgy offered a relief from the home-made quality of much nonconformist observance – the jollying along from the pulpit necessary in the absence of a prescribed sequence of events; the emphasis on the personality of the minister; the openness of extempore prayer to the insidious importation of contentious matter.

If the discovery of Evensong was my good fortune, my bad luck was to happen on the Prayer Book at a time of liturgical experimentation. The 8 am staple of the college chapel was the Series 2 Eucharist, and rather impressive it was – chiefly, I later found, because it was in some degree translucent to the older order which stood behind it. Series 3 I discovered hardly later than the Prayer Book. If it struck me as markedly inferior, I can at least claim immunity from one criticism often levelled at opponents of the new rite: my estimate was not simply a conservative preference for the known and cherished over the innovative and (as some would have it) exciting.

Not all the innovations struck me as objectionable. The reordering of events within the communion service – the removal of the Gloria

117

from its final position is, I suppose, the most frequently lamented case – jarred on no old habits of mine. I found it a curious point of view, though, which could argue for such changes on the grounds of ancient and Catholic precedent while urging, for other purposes, a thoroughgoing modernity. Rather more disturbing to me was the loss of good order – not all on account of the inconvenience inseparable from even the most needful change. Rooted in the Series 3 Eucharist, with its scope for free intercessions and its variety of options for both text and posture, there is a tendency to convert the priest not so much into a 'president' as into a master of ceremonies, directing the congregation with more or less tact and discretion, as his own taste may devise. It is less common than it used to be to find oneself in a communion service where the personality of the priest is only incidental. If Series 3 has been welcomed by many clergy, I am not certain that it has always been from the most disinterested of motives. Perhaps it is a prejudice to prefer an ordering of worship settled and strong enough to absorb the incidental distractions of time, place and personality; certainly, I can hardly argue that freedom from upset should be the ruling consideration. After all, the Prayer Book of 1662 was the upshot of a century's disturbance, and the occasion of more. Nevertheless there is surely some virtue in an order which testifies to the unchanging witness of the Church, if one can be had – though the very triviality of some of the changes introduced by the revisers suggests that they would not be inclined to agree.

All these reactions, however, were by the way compared with the main impression made on me by Series 3. Coming to it when my discovery of the Prayer Book was still so recent, I found the impoverishment of language breathtaking. In the arguments which have followed the introduction of Series 3, it may be that too much has been made out of the 'beauty' of the Prayer Book. Even the most committed advocates of the revised forms don't contend that they match 1662 in linguistic felicity. To argue strongly on the basis of 'beauty', then, is tactically inept – it attacks a position which has already been vacated, or never occupied. More dangerously, it encourages the riposte that a preference for the old forms of worship is merely an aesthetic matter, whereas the revisers have addressed themselves to matters of pastoral and theological substance, even urgency. How easy, then, to characterise a preference for the Prayer Book as a sort of self-indulgence, harmless enough if entertained in silence, but frivolously contentious if voiced. It was misgivings along these lines, at any rate, which at first encouraged me to contain my disappointment with the new liturgies. If the disappointment had been abated by evidence of any upsurge of new life, I dare say I would still be swallowing my objections; but the evidence I have seen is mixed. I have seen Series 3 happily adopted by flourishing congregations, with business proceeding much as usual. I have seen a weak congregation approach the point of collapse, though the causes which govern such things are too complex to assign the blame confidently to liturgical change. The evidence is, at best, uncertain, and my disappointment remains. What has hardened it into protest, though, is my increasing belief that the original impulse for liturgical reform fits into a disturbing pattern of ecclesiastical behaviour.

The pattern has been most clearly defined by Dr Edward Norman, in his book, *Church and Society in England, 1770–1970* (1976) – a penetrating study more warmly welcomed by Dr Norman's fellow historians than by his fellow priests. Throughout the period, he argues, the leading voices of the Church of England have tended to derive their views on current questions of social and political morality from the prevailing attitudes of the lay intelligentsia of the day. Instead of defining and developing a distinctively Christian view of such matters, they have on the whole contented themselves with secondhand versions of the current secular moral seriousness – and, as the currents of secular seriousness have shifted, each generation of churchmen has tended to identify the new ideas with essential Christianity, and to dismiss its predecessors as inexplicably deficient in prophetic understanding. Dr Norman explains the recurrent process in terms of the class and educational background of the clergy. Now as then, Anglican priests are drawn mainly from the educated middle class; now as then, their training is largely modelled on the traditional forms of higher education. This predisposes them to respect, and draw upon, ideas which emanate from the well-regarded professional intellectual disciplines (nowadays Economics, Psychology, Philosophy and, to an extent which would have made Marx and Weber blush, Sociology). But, largely untrained in these specialist areas, and ill-placed to form any independent assessment of the arguments current among the professionals, they are dependent on secondhand and vulgarised versions of the ideas for which they are avid. Thus the stock of ideas likely to commend itself to the more thoughtful of the clergy becomes indistinguishable from that up-market public opinion which 'quality' journalism exists to inform and purvey, while the leadership of the Church struggles to exhibit the fundamental consonance of Christian teaching with current enlightened consensus. It would be comforting to think of this tendency as an apologetic tactic, designed to shield the Church from the contempt of the well-placed and intellectually influential; among many of the clergy, however, it shows signs of being a rooted habit of mind. Uncritical adoption of the contents of contemporary moral seriousness is the deference vote delivered by the proletariat of the intelligentsia to the masters of advanced opinion.

It was in the 60s that the strength of this adaptive tendency was most vividly demonstrated. This was the decade in which atheistic humanism emerged as the dominant opinion of the intellectual community – and one might have thought that even the most advanced among Church leaders would have had a job swallowing that. But no, we have *Honest to God*, with God tentatively reconceived as 'the ground of our being', and 'situation ethics' offered as a substitute for traditional Christian morality – a perfect formula for adopting as Christians a whole segment of the intelligentsia who had rather hoped they were atheists. But the Bishop of Woolwich was the sign, not the cause, of the latest adaptation of the Church to fashionable opinion. The trend has been carried forward in journals, conferences, discussion groups and one knows not how many of the species of sermon described by the poet C. H. Sisson – 'so often no more than an exhortation to entertain more fervently that common stock of vague and politicised morality which is bandied about the world, day in, day out.' The direction of the trend is, by now, clear enough – and its contents are indeed politicised. The faithful are increasingly incited by leaders of the Church to regard the developed countries as guilty of a history of exploitation which renders them culpable for many of the difficulties now experienced by the Third World; they are exhorted to equate sin with oppressive economic structures, and to regard the structures of Capitalism as particularly oppressive; salvation is portrayed as inseparable from the collective solution of problems diagnosed as social; a doctrine of human rights, coloured by these political presuppositions, is prescribed as an essential component of the faith. I supply this catalogue of advanced clerical opinions not to dispute the particular conclusions, but to indicate the context in which the recent round of liturgical revisions took place. I don't suggest that the revisers themselves bear much resemblance to this identikit picture of the progressive priest – simply that they shared the general permeability to the wash of enlightened opinion as it filtered down through the strata of the intelligentsia in increasingly vapid and diluted form. If, in the 60s and 70s, the cutting edge of enlightened opinion has been characterised by some elements of genuine radicalism, the soft centre has been a mulch of vague progressive sentiment. Radicalism trickles down as easy cynicism about the value of national and social institutions, willing adoption of the most novel diagnoses of perennial problems, increased sympathy towards arguments for change and a tendency to justify values by reference to 'the community'. The impulse which led to the production of the Series 3 liturgies is presented as a discerning diagnosis of an impediment to the effective witness of the Church in the contemporary world. It should be seen, I believe, rather more as a conditioned response to the current (and, need one add, transient) contents of enlightened secular opinion. The results are neither radical nor prophetic, but modishly adaptive; they are the fruits of a misconceived theology of relevance.

The character of the adaptation is apparent enough. In the Eucharist, relative clauses give way to staccato imperatives – 'you take away the sin of the world: have mercy on us: you are seated at the right hand of the father: receive our prayer.' – immediacy is preferred to a developed literacy. The revised collects and Morning and Evening Prayer testify to the invincibility in our time of the argument for change, even where there is no more profound end in view than a bit of redecorating. In the Easter Anthems, 'Christ our passover is sacrificed for us: therefore let us keep the feast' becomes 'Christ our passover has been sacrificed for us: so let us celebrate the feast'. What improvement there so substantial as to justify the expense of printer's ink? Even the communal emphasis of politicised lay morality finds its wan reflection, in the 'We' of the new Creed and in the arrival in the confessions of that theological newcomer, sin 'through ignorance' – well-adapted to cover the unreconstructed naivety of most of the faithful in the matter of oppressive political and economic institutions.

It is here that language again enters the argument – not on the much-canvassed point of 'beauty', but as a fortification of the liturgy against the entry of attitudes whose chief commendation is their contemporary currency. It is the linguistic vacuity of Series 3 which makes it such a convenient receptacle for the spirit of the age. The Book of Common Prayer achieved its settled form in a period when the state of the language was more propitious than the present for liturgical enterprise. English was going through the phase of its greatest native energy while, for the learned, the digestion of Latin prose models and the educational emphasis on the study of rhetoric had opened up a new possibility of considered, consciously-structured written style. The result was a public language capable of incorporating the energy of common speech as well as the resources of formal style, and able to move between them with sureness of touch. A glance at the translations of the Bible produced in the eighteenth century is enough to show that this achievement was momentary; and in the twentieth century we have no comparable resources. Serious concern with the values of prose style is the province of few, even among writers. The native energy of common speech, subject in any case to the erosions of time and use, is cowed by the greater force of the language of mass communications. The possibility of originating a strong and versatile public language has vanished, at least for a season. We have instead a dissonant variety of styles and usages, with the stilted and deracinated language of official documents as the only remaining vestige of agreed public speech. When a proposal comes before us to render the liturgy into modern English, we do well to be sceptical, for the notion of 'modern English' is a convenient fiction. Revisers are obliged to choose, with no firm guide, from the rummage-stall of dialects on offer. As might have been expected, the resulting texts commute between the possibilities, with an embarrassed uncertainty in matters of detail. In the Te Deum, for instance, what principle of consistency reconciles the functionalist, unpunctuated bluntness of 'You are God we praise you' with the sham-antique of 'Throughout the world the holy Church acclaims you: Father of majesty unbounded'? In the Venite, we face the enfeebled colloquialism of 'If only you would hear his voice today', while the Magnificat presents us with a real curiosity: 'He has mercy on those who fear him: in ev'ry generation'. From what slim volume of Edwardian verse did that apostrophe spring to strike the revisers with the force of novelty? Of course it is easier to impugn the competence of the revisers than to face the awful likelihood that, in our day, this fruit salad is pretty much the best dish that can be confected from the ingredients to hand.

George Orwell, in his exposition of the Newspeak imposed by the authorities of 1984, pointed out that its function was to re-order the language so as to render certain notions unsayable, and finally unthinkable. My fear is that the reduced language of the new liturgies will have, inadvertently, something of the same effect if their use is allowed to become general – a range of spiritual insight embodied in a language stronger and more versatile than ours will become gradually less accessible. The process is not yet irreversible: but unless those who value the Prayer Book are prepared to voice their views, many more than me will have to wait a good deal longer than their eighteenth birthday to discover what it contains.

Everyone is caught in the decay of our speech, and the Church can only say what it has to say through language it has made its own. It was one of the great conquests of the sixteenth and seventeenth centuries that the Church commanded a language at once profound and familiar. Now, after immense deliberations, it injects trashy and unmeaningful speech even into the liturgy. There is no such thing as passing on profound truths in superficial speech.

C. H. SISSON
Poetry Nation Review, no. 2

A *friendly* view
PEGGY MAKINS

I have absolutely no right to take part in the controversy concerning the possible need for revision of the Church of England's Book of Common Prayer.

As a member of the Society of Friends, if I dare to address the Almighty rather than my fellow Quakers in Meeting for Worship, I must rely on spontaneous inspiration to provide both the words and the courage to utter them. Friends use no formulary; indeed there was a time when to read from a prayerbook would have been seen as trying to hide emptiness of thought behind a screen of convention.

My contribution to the argument, therefore, is the view seen through a window at the family squabble going on next door; invited but not to be taken seriously. Prayer to me was the means by which I was convinced of the existence of God and of His love for me and humanity; it was not formal prayer, led by a priest, but rather a series of yells for help which were answered if only I would listen and stop yelling.

In the Quaker mode of worship I found a sympathy with that listening which to me was lacking in other church services; the content rather than the package of a prayer was what mattered, the spirit rather than the letter, which gave heaven room to respond.

But, like Friends in general, I accept that people's ways to faith are many and varied, and the need for ritual and poetry is a real need and must be satisfied when it is felt. None of us would criticise the use of programmed ceremonies as part of the belief of the Church of England – and I would now see the Book of Common Prayer as a splendid luxury, to be valued as I value a cathedral or Michelangelo's Pietá, and impossible to replace.

When I go to church services, usually Evensong or Morning Prayer, occasionally Holy Communion as a spectator, I prefer the 1662 rites as a matter of course. It is not until now, when I am trying to add something to this discussion, that I have begun to wonder why.

Part of the reason is easy; like almost everyone else I resent having to change habits, particularly if I think they are not bad habits. Why should I have to learn new responses, listen to different invocations? What was wrong with the old ones? 'Nothing' said a patient social worker friend, 'except that two-thirds of the people who take part in the services you are familiar with don't understand what they're saying.'

But do the new prayers and responses make understanding any easier? In trying to clarify the complexity of our relationship with the deity, do we not attempt what is impossible? As a Friend, I know I ought to prefer plain speaking to mumbo-jumbo, and the simplicity of Series 3 to the richness of prayerbook language.

Silence, though, which I find so rewarding, is not simply blank silence, not just an absence of sound. It is made dense with mystery out of which, if I wait patiently enough, God will give me a prayer or a message to ponder on. If I try to explain the mystery, only the most splendid and elaborate phrases come to mind which convey that God is both awful and beautiful, but above all incomprehensible. So if two-thirds of worshippers don't understand what they are saying, they are sharing the cloud of unknowing with those priests and theologians whose expertise has taught them that God is beyond human understanding. Even when we repeat the central prayer of the whole Christian family, the Lord's Prayer, we are probably only imperfectly aware of what it means. But we can still use it as a prayer, and we can go on for a lifetime exploring its phrases and finding new, deeper meanings.

My mother taught me to say 'Our father which art in heaven' long before I knew what the words meant, and I never thought about it afterwards until I found out through experience that prayers are answered.

So what had I been meaning when I murmured 'Our Father' so often at school and in church; what had Jesus's words been saying all those years?

The puzzles begin quite early on: 'Thy kingdom come, thy will be done in earth as it is in heaven'. By the way, why change 'in earth' to 'on earth'? We talk about living in Britain, don't we? But going back to the whole phrase, surely 'Thy will' *is* done in earth, if God is truly all-powerful, all-wise, all-good, and the maker of all things? The source of everything is the source of all willpower, there is no other will to use; we are just given a share in it, as it were, and it is so potent that we feel as if we are captains of our souls. It may seem to me that I'm defying the Almighty, but as the pattern works out, it becomes clear that His will is being done even through my rebellion. So what is the difference between God's will being done on earth and done in heaven?

As many better than I am must have done, I thrashed this over in my mind for a long time; I prayed about it, as I was saying the Lord's Prayer. I asked to be given an explanation of something which seemed contradictory. I read a great many books by experts. And I don't suppose for a moment that the answer I eventually received will satisfy everybody or indeed most people. I have learned that the answers to prayers are individual answers; to publish them is to risk discord, because viewing a problem from a completely different angle can go so much against the grain.

So I offer my explanation of that phrase in fear and trembling, yet in confidence, because for me it rings true.

Consider, said the message, how things are in heaven. You, as a human being, don't really know whether the gates are of pearl or the streets of gold, but you believe that its inhabitants have the great and splendid certainty of knowing they are in paradise. Angels, cherubim, seraphim, all know they are perfectly secure in the love of the Almighty who cares for them and forever fills them with new life. They are free from all doubt, need nothing more.

That is where their situation differs from ours. If we too could know that we are inhabitants of God's kingdom, in his protection for eternity, what would that knowledge do for us?

First, our ideas about suffering would change, because the view before us would lengthen out far beyond human death; we should see that the agony, the cruelty, the illnesses and disabilities, and the bitter sorrows which go with them, are as necessary to our eternal welfare as the pains of labour are to the triumph of childbirth, or the strain and anxiety of hard striving before we pass an examination or reach the summit of a mountain.

Second, we should know that even if we never reached a mountain peak, never escaped from a handicap, God would understand the part we had to play and see our failings as needful to the whole drama. We would fear neither the destruction of the world nor the day of judgment; the trouble is our ignorance.

Some saints have indeed suspected they inhabited God's kingdom on earth. Remember the Lady Julian of Norwich saying, 'All shall be well, all shall be well, and all manner of things shall be well'. I think she knew she was in heaven already.

The Lord's Prayer has linked together Christians of all churches and no church for as long as belief in Christ has persisted. It is easy to mutter through the words and see in them a general desire for human good, but once you begin to think over what you are saying, you begin also to see how much light they shed on the character of Jesus, his understanding of us men and women, and his deep relationship with God, his heavenly father.

'Give us this day our daily bread', he said.

That seems simple enough. We need food, it keeps us alive, to want it is not wrong or unspiritual. But Jesus, as a man, recognises how much food can come to mean, say to a person who has had to go hungry pretty often. That man will start a day worrying about getting enough to eat, wondering whether perhaps a job will come his way or whether he will have to face the risk of stealing to get a crust. Or take the case of someone who has never gone hungry in his life, but who is a bit of a glutton; he can easily lose a morning pondering what to order for lunch, and thumbing through a wine list as he considers laying down an extra stock of claret.

Jesus thoroughly disapproved of spending a lot of time brooding about food. Maybe the women in his life had been perpetually asking everyone what they fancied for next week's joint. God, he said, knows quite well that human beings must eat; if He supplies enough for the birds, surely He'll not let men and women starve.

He had little sympathy with other homely anxieties either, such as having, as we say, nothing to wear. 'Consider the lilies', he said, 'how they grow; even Solomon in all his glory was not arrayed like one of these.' Lilies don't work, though, or scrimp and save to make themselves gorgeous, they trust God. So why on earth couldn't his fellows, the chosen people, trust God too?

He knew they couldn't trust God, as we can't; their faith and ours is not that great, so in his prayer he asked for bread: bread enough for only today. Enough to keep you alive and alert at present, not enough to let you sit back and stop striving.

What had come before the petition for bread had been that other phrase: 'Thy kingdom come'. This was what Jesus wanted everyone who followed him to put first, the rule of love which, if only folk would obey it, he knew would solve all the practical problems in the world.

Very few, of course, have ever really believed this, at least none of us ordinary people who may make sacrifices for *our* children, but not for anyone else's. And too often our motive for making no plans for tomorrow is the lazy hope that someone else will come along and give us what we need without our having to work for it.

The Jesus plan would mean going out and working hard for everyone but yourself, fortifying your soul with prayer, taking only your bare needs and being rewarded by the sight of others made happier or healthier through your efforts. I fear that most of us, including myself, aren't selfless enough to try it.

But those who yield up all they have find it succeeds marvellously. People like Mother Teresa of Calcutta, Salvation Army members, uncountable relief workers, social workers, nameless volunteers in whose hearts happiness grows like a rose against a sunny wall.

I must admit that one of the up-to-date alterations which the Church of England has decided to make in the Lord's Prayer makes me rather rebellious. 'Forgive us our trespasses, as we forgive them that trespass against us' are the old words, easy to remember and with just that hint of extra meaning to inspire thought. 'Forgive us our sins as we forgive those who sin against us' is far too cut and dried and much harder to say sincerely I find.

'Trespass' I translate as stepping on my preserves, possibly by accident, like someone inadvertently using my garden path as a short cut or sitting in my reserved seat in a train. I can get very offended about this sort of thing, especially if I'm in a bad mood at the time, but it soon gets forgotten and I would never dream of harbouring bad feeling against the person who did it. I would expect to be forgiven myself if I strayed into private premises or gatecrashed a stranger's wedding reception.

But I must admit that if someone in genuine malice sinned against me, stole my money, bashed me on the head, cheated me of some important right, I'd find it terribly hard to forgive, at least for a very long time. *Sin* to me is in the intention of the sinner; it's the strong urge to do me down. *Trespass* is slighter; it may be mischievous, thoughtless, but it's forgivable. So the traditional version of the prayer I find credible; the new makes much greater demands – and how can I ask God to forgive me when I doubt if I can forgive the one who sins against me?

What takes my breath away is the high moral level it puts us on; it compares us to God rather to God's disadvantage, as if Christ were saying: 'You can't sit up there stony-faced, Dad, when your own children are forgiving each other. At least be as kind as they are.'

So there are two puzzles. First, Jesus assumed we are of a forgiving nature, when he knew perfectly well that we aren't. So did he hope that by making us say over and over again that we forgive each other perhaps we would ultimately be less ready to hate, swear revenge and cherish grudges? The old Jehovah, after all, had specialised in revenge and never-forgotten wrongs – his bloody retaliation on the foes of the children of Israel was part of the history taught to every Jew, and Christ must have hoped his people would move from that primeval vindictiveness into the climate of love.

Perhaps the other thing he had in mind was that true forgiveness understands why the trespass was committed in the first place. 'You stole my purse,' a mother might say, 'because your friends were all going out and you couldn't bear to be left lonely at home, and perhaps have them jeer at your poverty. I know how you felt, I might have done the same thing at your age; but don't do it again.'

Understanding is better than forgiveness; it can restore affection between a trespasser and his victim. But can we expect no more mercy than we give? This is the nub of the telling phrase, the dig at our self-confidence which should make us look again at our daily behaviour, the way we feel about our neighbours and everyone we meet. If we are loving our neighbours as ourself, or even trying to, we have little to fear. But if we are a mass of pride and egotism, then what hope have we? 'You get what you give' is an old warning implied in the Lord's Prayer. I think we ignore it at our peril.

To work your way through the Lord's Prayer as if it were something utterly new, and at the same time to pray to be enlightened about its many shades of meaning results often in being stopped in your tracks, as I'm stopped in mine when I come to 'And lead us not into temptation, but deliver us from evil.' A fine God he must be, you might think, to condemn sin and warn us of his wrath if we transgress, then deliberately decoy us into wrongdoings so that he can drop thunderbolts on us. What sort of behaviour is that, for goodness sake?

Well, the new translators have tried to solve the riddle by saying 'Do not bring us to the time of trial', but most of us can't forget the old version which speaks so clearly to the human condition. I'm glad Jesus mentions temptation as if he'd felt it; this is something men and women know well, wondering if our decision, say, concerning our children's education was unselfish or being tempted to follow a principle rather than think of their good, or whether going on holiday, for instance, is just self-indulgence or really justified.

Probably the most virtuous feel the most guilt; certainly there's plenty of yielding to temptation nowadays when so many people don't seem able to drink without becoming alcoholics, smoke without damaging their lungs, or take a headache pill without becoming a drug addict. Are the good things in life just traps set by the Almighty to keep up the supply of Hell-fodder? Have we reached a stage where we must give up all enjoyment in case it corrupts us?

'Lead us not into temptation' – but surely the mind and reason we have been given to control our appetites, these too are good things? There have been and still are puritanical sects who forbid music, dancing, feasting and revelling, but they've not eradicated temptation. With them it has taken the form of making them feel superior to other people, which is the worst temptation of all. Better gluttony than pride any day I say. But still wouldn't it be simpler to pray 'Lead us out of temptation', thus straightening out that awkward 'not into'? And avoiding the complicated 'being brought to the time of trial' which appears to introduce the Day of Judgment into what is otherwise a homely, intimate personal talk with God?

Jesus's relationship with his heavenly father was trusting, affectionate, unafraid – one only wishes every human parental relationship could be the same. He addressed the Lord, we are told, as 'Dad' rather than Almighty God, and spoke spontaneously – and it occurs to me that in the famous Jewish musical, 'Fiddler on the Roof', the Milkman, Tevye, does exactly the same sort of thing.

'Lord,' says Tevye, 'I know there's no disgrace in being a poor man, but there's no great honour either . . .' And suddenly I could hear Jesus, another young Jew, saying, 'And, dad, if you love us, don't actually put temptation in our way, will you? Just get on delivering us from evil . . .' Now if only we had the same trust, the same closeness to God, might we not too be delivered from evil? There is something to be said, then, for leaving the words of the Lord's Prayer alone. They are familiar, they are a point of union for Christians of all denominations, and they can inspire us to think more deeply about what we say and what we believe. And the same argument could be applied to the rest of the liturgy. Maybe if the Prayer Book is to be revised, it should be made even more poetic and visionary; the figure of Christ, at once so human and simultaneously so superhuman can be glimpsed, it seems, only through the loving imagination. He is like a picture painted by an Impressionist; approach it closely and it seems like nothing more than a collection of dots, dashes and squiggles, but stand away and half close the eyes, and a portrait of love incarnate can be seen. A Book of Common Prayer which made it seem that worshipping, which nourishes the soul and spirit, is as simple and straightforward as cooking food which nourishes the body would be misleading.

But should ancient rites then never be changed? If they continue to produce an appetite for goodness, perhaps not. In one of Thor Heyerdahl's books about Easter Island, he writes that copies of a very sacred book were kept among the holy objects in the most secret caves of the islanders. Nobody knew exactly what the book contained, it was so long since anyone had been instructed in the ancient sacred language, but in the opinion of native authorities, the first page was the holiest of all. Great efforts were made to translate its wording, and finally it was agreed that the gist of its teaching was 'When this page begins to show wear, copy it exactly and put it in place of the old one.' The words didn't matter; the awe it inspired had increased as its incomprehensibility had deepened.

Would the Book of Common Prayer be an even mightier aid to worship if it finally became a collection of sacred sounds and syllables?

There are two other points I'd like to make. This first one I approach circumspectly because I share the Quaker belief in the priesthood of all believers, and the surplus nature of professional priests. (Incidentally, one of the reasons why I deplore the eagerness of some women to be ordained is that I always hoped women had enough commonsense to see that the idea of a person licensed to act as a go-between between God and man is outdated. To pay people to be social workers, teachers and, maybe, healers – that is a different matter, and I'm for it. To imagine, though, that you can give them the exclusive power to forgive sins seems to me wild.) Going back, though, to a professional priesthood and, therefore, a profession of theologians serving an organised, authoritarian church – I ask myself, what do the theologians find to do? Many of them claim that all truth has already been revealed, so there are no new discoveries in waiting; most write learned and delightful books justifying God's ways to man, or, of course, trying to fit God into a scientifically dying universe.

But when all that has been done, there remains the fabric of a church to be shored up, renewed, rebuilt or pulled down. Part of the fabric of the Church of England is the Book of Common Prayer. I can never remember a time when it wasn't being revised in some way or another. When I was married I agreed to obey my husband, in the hope that I might at some time or other be able to blame him for any disaster in our life; but many brides were plumping for 'cherish', which was the current subject of controversy. Prayer-book revision disagreements do make publicity, which the Church feels it needs. Does it therefore take care to keep them going?

Finally, does the mediocre automatically drive out the good? If the new revisers have their way will we lose forever the 1662 liturgy? I doubt it. There was a time in the theatre when actor-managers started rewriting Shakespeare, or getting hack authors to do it for them. We had a happy-ending *King Lear*, a bowdlerised *Antony and Cleopatra*, 'dashing the bottle from his toothless gums' rather than 'the nipple' was the memorable improvement Bowdler put forward in *Macbeth*, a Cibberised *Hamlet*. Purist critics howled in anguish, but they needn't have bothered. Shakespeare himself was soon back again.

And I believe that if the time-honoured Book of Common Prayer is really the best we can do to codify Christian church worship, it will never be entirely lost or forgotten – though it may have to share a place on the pew shelf with a few alternatives. It was, I am certain, created with love and the best of intentions, and is the kind of thing which carries an atmosphere of heaven about it, like mother-love. Only if it ever ceases to convey the slightest hint of God's meaning to His worshippers will it become obsolete, and in that case there will be no tragedy. It is, though, much more likely to prove indestructible.

Why are the clergy . . .?

Why are the clergy of the Church of England
Always altering the words of the prayers in the Prayer
 Book?
Cranmer's touch was surer than theirs, do they not
 respect him?
For instance last night in church I heard
(I italicise the interpolation)
'The Lord bless you and keep you *and all who are dear
 unto you*'
As the blessing is a congregational blessing and meant
 to be
This is questionable on theological grounds
But is it not offensive to the ear and also ludicrous?
That 'unto' is a particularly ripe piece of idiocy
Oh how offensive it is. I suppose we shall have next
'Lighten our darkness we beseech thee oh Lord *and
 the darkness of all who are dear unto us.*'
It seems a pity. Does Charity object to the objection?
Then I cry, and not for the first time to that smooth
 face
Charity, have pity.

STEVIE SMITH

Faith and song
SYDNEY CARTER

Faith, and not belief, is the life blood of a hymn; which is why so many unbelievers, or only half believers, can still sing and enjoy a hymn. By 'faith' I mean the reaching out, in hope and trust, in love and celebration, to the source of all we are, and of all that makes our life worth living. The Christian name for that is 'God', but you can still love and trust and celebrate whether you call it 'God' or not.

By 'belief' I mean the intellectual acceptance of a particular theology. In the case of Christianity you have to accept more than a philosophy; you have to believe that certain events took place about two thousand years ago. Whether they did or didn't there is no way of proving unless we can invent a time machine and travel back to see. But unless you can believe that Jesus actually lived, and rose up from the dead, you can hardly call yourself a Christian.

Mere 'belief', admittedly, is not enough. You must have faith as well. You must rejoice in and celebrate what you believe has happened. 'The devils also believe, and tremble' wrote James. What the devils lacked was faith. They could believe it happened, but were sorry that it did. That is what I understand James to be saying.

Confronted by the claims of official Christianity (Baptist, Catholic, Anglican or Orthodox) what most people lack today is not the faith, but the belief. All men of good will have a modicum of faith. You do not have to be a Christian to have it, and you do not have to be a Christian to write or sing a hymn. In *Speaking of Siva* (Penguin Classics) are some passionate and startling songs of praise and celebration. They are addressed, not to Jesus, but to Shiva. In the Bible itself, in the Psalms, are some of the best hymns ever written. They are all pre-Christian.

But it is with Christian hymns (I take it) that we are concerned in a book like this: the kind that can be found in *Hymns Ancient and Modern* or *The English Hymnal*. The question to be asked – the question I ask myself, at any rate – is this: dare I sing them, as an expression of my faith, even though I question the theology?

The simple answer is, I do. Nothing will stop me singing '*St Patrick's Breastplate*,' even though I may not believe, implicitly, everything St Patrick did. Does this make me a hypocrite? If it

134

does, a hypocrite I shall remain – a cheerful, singing hypocrite – until such time, if such a time shall ever be, when I am able to believe everything St Patrick could. Meanwhile I am content to let the wheat of faith and the tares – if tares they turn out to be – of my doubt grow up together.

I have used the word 'hypocrite' advisedly. According to my dictionary it comes from the Greek word for an actor. This reflects the attitude of official Christianity to any kind of 'make-believe'. St Augustine was suspicious of the theatre; the Puritans thought it downright devilish. In the Middle Ages, some concession had been made: there was a form of Christian drama, in which the life and deeds of Jesus (or of Noah) could be represented on a kind of stage, providing they were represented as being literally true. In the English mystery plays some liberty was allowed with minor characters – shepherds and the like; there was even clowning, but the actors had to tread carefully. There was a danger that the character called 'Vice' might steal the show, and this was frowned upon. The main characters had to keep closely to the Gospel plot.

A dramatic production like *Jesus Christ Superstar*, which raises, and does not answer, the question of whether Jesus was really what he thought he was, or the Church taught he was, would have been regarded as, literally, diabolical. Tim Rice and Andrew Lloyd Webber would have been in danger of being burnt alive.

But today they can ask that question with impunity. Indeed, the Church is, on the whole, obliged to them for asking it. It shows, at any rate, that somebody is interested; it is better than being ignored altogether. And so it came about that the first time I heard the score of *Jesus Christ Superstar* was in the Church of St Thomas Aquinas, Toronto, with Rice and Webber there in person to answer any questions that anyone might care to put.

Not all Christians, it is true, have been so hospitable. There are those who feel that Jesus belongs to them and that the interpretation of the gospel is their monopoly. But is it? There is a growing feeling outside the official body (or bodies) of the Church that Jesus belongs to anybody who can get (or be got by) Jesus, and that this can happen without the blessing of the Church. That Christ, in fact, is too important to be left to the Christians.

Tim Rice and Andrew Lloyd-Webber, neither of whom could call himself a Christian, are not the only ones to attempt a new interpretation of the Gospel story. The authors of *Godspell* were not Christian either. Dennis Potter also was not Christian when he wrote *Son of Man*, which shocked so many Christian and non-Christian viewers, though I believe he has become more Christian since. In

Son of Man there were no songs. For a Dennis Potter play with songs we had to wait for *Pennies from Heaven*. None of the songs were hymns by any stretch of the imagination; they were all pop songs current in the nineteen-thirties. Yet by an amazing *tour de force* they were used to achieve what I would consider a religious purpose. Man's vision of the Glory – one does not have to say 'of God', but for a Christian it would be that – and his falling short of it, is what *Pennies from Heaven* was about. What *Pennies from Heaven* shows, is that song – almost any kind of song – can be made to serve a religious purpose, if *it is presented in the right context*. The converse is also true: any kind of song, however holy, can be made to serve a purpose that is diabolical. 'The Old Rugged Cross' sung to sanctify a lynching party, would be a case in point. Heretics have been burnt to the sound of holy music.

The avowed purpose of a hymn, however it may be misused, is to praise a god: a fact which is strangely commemorated in the word itself. It is derived from Hymen, the Greek god of marriage: the God it praised was Hymen himself, and what he stood for. A hymn (*humen*), says Eric Partridge in *Origins*, was a bridal song – 'perhaps originally the cry greeting the announcement of virginity removed'.

The singing of hymns – as distinct from the singing of anthems or motets – is something in which the congregation is expected to take part. A hymn, therefore, should not be too difficult to sing. It should also not be too difficult to understand. Above all, it should be something to which those who are singing should be able to say 'Amen' – 'so be it' – with an easy conscience. A hymn whose words are likely to shock or divide the congregation, or leave them wondering what exactly they have said 'Amen' to, is not really suitable. This would exclude nearly all the songs in *Jesus Christ Superstar*. They might serve the aims of religion in other ways, but not as hymns. At least two of the songs in *Godspell* – 'Day by Day' and 'Come and prepare ye the way of the Lord' – would qualify, and are occasionally used as hymns.

Songs which can command a safe Amen from *all* the congregation are becoming rarer – whether they are old or newly written. In 'All things Bright and Beautiful' few now feel happy about singing:

> The rich man in his castle,
> The poor man at the gate,
> God made them, high or lowly,
> And ordered their estate.

Even 'Onward Christian Soldiers' I have heard objected to, and this was fifty years ago. 'Verse three will be omitted' the vicar said, 'because it simply isn't true. It says "We are not divided" – but we *are* divided. Protestants cannot agree with Catholics. Catholics cannot agree with Protestants. Verse three will not be sung.' No sermon has so stunned me or stuck in my memory as this brief announcement from the pulpit. A hymn *not true?* Then why was it in the book? It was as if the vicar had said that something in the Bible was not true.

If words in the old hymn books have had their critics, words in the new hymn books have even more. LITTLE RED HYMN-BOOK said a headline in the *Daily Express* when in 1971 Galliard brought out *New Life*. Too many items, it seemed, betrayed a left-wing point of view. Which were singled out, I can't remember. Looking through the book I find several that blame the rich for being selfish and few that criticise the poor; but I seem to remember that there was the same bias in the words of Jesus. The chief crime of these new songs seemed to be their topicality. As poetry, some were open to criticism; some of the new ones were sentimental, like the old ones, but in a different way. The language of protest has its clichés, like the older language of orthodoxy. The new is slangier, the old is stuffier. Only one song was accused of blasphemy. That one was by me. It was a song about the crucifixion, in which one of the two thieves crucified with Jesus launches an attack on God:

> You can blame it on to Adam,
> You can blame it on to Eve,
> You can blame it on the Apple,
> But that I can't believe.
> It was God who made the Devil,
> And the Woman, and the Man,
> And there wouldn't be an Apple
> If it wasn't in the plan.
> 'It's God they ought to crucify,
> Instead of you and me',
> I said to the carpenter
> A-hanging on the tree.

This is not the sort of thing to which the congregation will automatically say 'Amen'. It fails, therefore, to be a hymn. But it was not meant to be a hymn, as I would define a hymn. That does not mean that it could not be used in church (or out) to promote an attitude of worship. In this song, no answer is given to the thief's attack. Its purpose is to shock the listener into finding an honest answer for himself. He has the Bible and the teaching of the church to help him. His inner faith should come up with an answer. The purpose of this song is to promote that faith, homoeopathically. If it can achieve that purpose then it will have praised God, in a backhanded way.

The same, I think, would be said of the songs given to Pilate, Herod and Judas in *Jesus Christ Superstar*. Within the context of a play, or even of an oratorio, this is understood. Someone has to play the villain or the drama will collapse. When Pilate brings Jesus before the rabble, someone must shout 'Crucify him!' To use a song like this is to use it like a character in a drama. But that is not the usual way to use song in a hymn-book. What congregations tend to look for, in a hymn, is a simple and straightforward statement of the truth. But to state the truth is not, necessarily, to *convey* the truth. To do that, it may sometimes be wiser to deny the truth. This is a method which Zen Buddhist teachers have been long aware of. The important thing is to make somebody see the truth for himself, no matter how you do it.

Behind the belief that a hymn can tell the truth, easily – not the whole of the truth, perhaps, but certainly nothing *but* the truth – lies the belief in some kind of infallibility, whether of the Bible or the Pope. For many who genuinely seek the truth – the sort of truth that religion is concerned with – such a belief is no longer possible. For such as these, the sort of song that serves the truth indirectly, that forces them to find the truth, may be a more effective way to worship than the good, old-fashioned hymn that assumes, on the part of the worshippers, beliefs they may no longer have.

Is this a defeatist attitude? Only if you feel that the beliefs in question matter more than the faith which they support and which sometimes seems to get along without them. And doubt itself can be a form of faith, if only in the value of the truth. 'Christ', wrote Simone Weil in a letter to a friend, 'likes us to prefer truth to him, because before being Christ he is Truth.' If this bold claim is correct – and I defy a Christian to contradict it – then the true hymns of our time may be those songs of faithful questioning which do not seem to qualify as hymns at all.

God, who does not dwell on high
In the wide, unwinking sky,
And whose quiet counsels start
Simply from the human heart,

Teach us strong and teach us true
What to say and what to do,
That we love as best we can
All Thy creatures. Even man.
                    Amen.

CHARLES CAUSLEY
from 'On Being Asked to write a School Hymn'

A college sermon*

BRYAN THWAITES

Today is the second Sunday after Easter, and so the pomp and pageantry and splendour of the services of Easter Sunday are still vivid in our minds. Wherever we might have worshipped that morning – my parish church (as I call it) is the great Cathedral of Winchester where the sights and sounds of any great festival are almost mind-blowing – we came away uplifted and renewed by the wonder of the Resurrection.

So that would have been a very natural theme for me on this *first* Sunday of our Summer Term here, and I nearly fell for it, especially as today I am breaking with my own thirteen-year-old tradition here of sermonising on the *last* Sunday of the academic year. But then I remembered that I have always spoken especially for those who are about to leave the uniquely protective academic world for the primitive jungle (for that is what it is) of society at large; and my theme has usually been some concept or notion which has seemed, to me at least, to have been of particular concern or interest to students during the year.

Today, however, I am throwing all those rationalisations to the wind. Instead, I am going to particularise on one event of our year here so far, and then to draw a few brief generalisations from it.

That event was our annual Maynard-Chapman Memorial Divinity Lecture, last term, given by the eminent Professor Dunstan of King's College (and former tutor of our own gifted Chaplain), as the climax of that splendid week of celebration of the fiftieth anniversary of the inauguration of this Chapel. I confess to a great disappointment that so few of our students were there – indeed, I further confess to my great puzzlement that so few students take advantage of the intellectual stimulation that so many distinguished visiting scholars offer right here on the campus – for that lecture of his was a *tour de force*, as well as a *tour d'horizon*, with the title '1929–1979: And What Have the Righteous Done?'

The one – and only one – point of his that I am now going to

---

* This contribution is to be read more as oratory than literature: for it is reproduced exactly as delivered in the chapel of Westfield College on Sunday, 29 April 1977, before a congregation of students.

elaborate relates to what 'the righteous' have done to the Anglican liturgy during these fifty years – or more exactly, during the last fourteen years under the Prayer Book (Alternative and Other Services) Measure 1965 (to an academic audience: always quote your references!).

Not a bad place to start with is what is possibly the most reverent moment in the Eucharist – the Sanctus (which, incidentally, has inspired some of the greatest music ever composed: if you do not know, for example, Bach's setting of it in his 'B Minor Mass', then your education still has at least one gap in it). Listen carefully to what many of us have already said earlier this morning, whether we were at the Roman Mass or Anglican Eucharist:

> Holy, holy, holy Lord,
> God of power and might,
> Heaven and earth are full of your glory.

and now to what your predecessors would have said twenty years ago:

> Holy, holy, holy,
> Lord God of hosts,
> Heaven and earth are full of thy glory:
> Glory be to thee,
> O Lord most High. Amen.

You may say that the difference is not very marked and perhaps you would be right. Perhaps, too, that Series 3 version will eventually come to seem to you as natural and euphonious as the 1662 version does to me. But, given more time, I would argue in detail that there has been a pointless decline in aesthetic style with no gain at all in understanding, and that this is shown up much more markedly in another prayer inherent in Christian worship: the Confession. Listen again to something which we all said together only fifteen minutes ago:

> Almighty God, our heavenly Father, we have sinned against you and against our fellow men, in thought and word and deed, in the evil we have done, and in the good we have not done, through ignorance, through weakness, through our own deliberate fault. . . .

I find it jolly difficult to be 'truly sorry and repent' through the medium of such dreary and abbreviated blank verse. How can anyone fail to agree that the earlier version not only says it with so much greater reverence and ease?

Almighty God, Father of our Lord Jesus Christ, Maker of all things, Judge of all men; We acknowledge and bewail our manifold sins and wickedness, Which we, from time to time, most grievously have committed, By thought, word, and deed, Against thy Divine Majesty, Provoking most justly thy wrath and indignation against us. . . .

and then comes the repeated cry of the repentant soul:

We do earnestly repent, And are heartily sorry for these our misdoings; The remembrance of them is grievous unto us; The burden of them is intolerable. Have mercy upon us, Have mercy upon us, most merciful Father; For Thy son our Lord Jesus Christ's sake, Forgive us all that is past. . . .

When I have said that, I really feel as though I have got something off my chest!

Have no fear – I am not going on with these direct comparisons which, even for the Anglican Communion service, let alone the Anglican Matins and Evensong, would take the rest of the day. But I urge you at least to compare and study the old and the new, and in doing so, ask yourselves questions like these:

Does a modern idiom really help spiritual exercise?

And how modern is modern? – for idiomatic usage is changing remarkably rapidly nowadays.

Contrariwise: is there not much to be said for a liturgy which, in its constancy, matches the eternal and unchanging nature of God Himself?

Is brevity – no, not the soul of wit; is brevity an end in itself?

Or: Does not repetition, either of words and phrases or of ideas, give the mind time to grasp and contemplate the meaning?

Are not beauty and seemliness entirely desirable and proper attributes of divine worship?

Is there no room for subtlety and allusion? (And here, I again refer to the old phrase 'holy, holy, holy', with its clear reference to the Trinity – imperiously emphasised by the triplets of the Bach setting which I have already mentioned—and compare it with the hopeless mess of the Series 3 'holy, holy, holy Lord.')

By now, it will be obvious to you how much importance I attach to the way in which ideas are communicated by language. In the particular context of the liturgy, great importance should surely be attached as well to a familiarity with all the standard and historical texts. The Bible, I suppose we would all agree, goes without saying and any serious Christian will read it regularly. But let me give you just two examples of what I believe your generation is missing because of the emphasis which 'the righteous' of my generation have given to the Eucharist. Perhaps some ecclesiastical pendulum was bound to swing, but at least in the Anglican Church, the rites of Morning and Evening Prayer have fallen virtually into desuetude.

Consider first the Psalms in the metrical form as originally given in the Translation of the great English Bible used in the time of Henry VIII, and as still printed in the Book of Common Prayer. They comprise what is called the Psalter and they are so arranged that they are read (or sung) in their entirety in each and every month of the year. Now the Psalter not merely comprehends the whole gamut of pre-Christian theology on which Christianity itself is based, not merely expresses the spectrum of human emotion from the depths of despair to the heights of spiritual sensation, not merely exerts a discipline on one's own daily prayer. In addition, the means with which it serves these ends is a sublimity of language which has never been surpassed in the English tongue. And when, moreover, they are sung in what is commonly called our English Cathedral tradition, the aesthetic and the spiritual combine to an extent which can all too easily bring tears to eyes as though blinded by God's own presence.

But how many of you know your Psalms well? How many have heard them day after day? What have the righteous done to deny you this incomparable gift? And as a fourth question, no longer rhetorical, who amongst you could give any context to such marvellous verses as:

The earth is the Lord's, and all that therein is:
the compass of the world and they that dwell therein.

The Lord is my light, and my salvation;
whom then shall I fear:
the Lord is the strength of my life;
of whom then shall I be afraid?

Some put their trust in chariots, and some in horses:
but we will remember the Name of the Lord our God.

Keep innocency, and take heed unto the thing that is right:
for that shall bring a man peace at the last.

Be wise now therefore, O ye kings:
be learned, ye that are judges of the earth.

Like as the hart desireth the water-brooks:
so longeth my soul after thee, O God.

(What a searing cry is that: just listen again –

Like as the hart desireth the water-brooks:
so longeth my soul after thee, O God.)

And, as a final one:

Let every thing that hath breath:
praise the Lord.

Who can place that?

All that I have just said about the Psalms carries over identically
to the collects. Every day, a Christian priest will say, usually by
himself, his evening office; so every day an Anglican priest will say
three collects of which the third is . . . how many of you could
stand up and say it? . . . one of the shortest yet most moving prayers
ever written:

Lighten our darkness, we beseech thee O Lord; and by thy great
mercy defend us from all perils and dangers of this night; for the
love of thy only Son, our Saviour, Jesus Christ. Amen.

I often say that to myself, in all sorts of places and at all sorts of
times; and I do so not only by way of prayer, but because it has,
rather like a fine diamond, so many facets to it, each radiating its
own brilliance.

Now for generalisations (and about time too, you'll be thinking).

The most obvious question is this: what are the circumstances
which justify changes in existing practices? – a question which goes
far beyond religious practice: one, indeed, which lies at the heart of
the vast play now being enacted on the national stage under the title
General Election. But let me restrict my answer to the practice of
Christianity.

First, despite an earlier inference which you may have drawn at
the time – that eternal truths might imply unvarying practice –
change is surely an inescapable quality of God's own creation. This
is obviously true of the physical Universe; and as for the human
race, the gift of Free Will, if nothing else, ensures change. So it
would be absurd either to expect, or to attempt to ensure, that
religious practice remains invariable from one generation to another.

But the very use of that liturgical phrase 'from one generation to another' suggests an inadequate model of what either does or should happen in society as a whole. Except within a family, the so-called generations are as continuous as time itself – like an ever-rolling stream (context again, please!) – and my interpretation of history is that it takes some external and generation-free influence to effect changes in practice as radical as those manifested in Series 3. Never mind, then, how those changes came about: I am more interested in when we shall be confronted with Series 4! On this, I find the Church of England's Liturgical Commission's own commentary of 1971 rather ambivalent. Its chairman writes:

> Inevitably the question is bound to arise, 'What next? We have had Series 1, 2, and 3. How many more experimental services must we endure?' The answer will, I hope, be reassuring. It is our desire to regard Series 3 as definitive . . . we hope we shall not be obliged to undertake yet another major piece of revision.

Well, I hope so too! But equally I am not at all reassured, as he hopes, by the thought of Series 3 being definitive. You will have already gathered that I think it is pretty awful, and I guess that, easily within the lifetime of all of us here including myself, enough people will agree with my assessment to make further change irresistible.

The lesson to be drawn from this confusing state of affairs is plain, and is twofold. Don't change well-known practices unless there are very compelling reasons for doing so; and when you do change, then ensure – to plagiarise a phrase of Cardinal Newman's which I have quoted before in this place – that a new development is true and conservative of what has gone before it.

My second generalisation I will just state without proof, as mathematicians sometimes say. It is a form of inverted snobbery to think that one's personal or communal worship is enhanced by putting it in an as ordinary or everyday setting as possible – by reverting, so to speak, to the Roman catacombs. On the contrary, it is the experience of the ages that the cleanliness of the altar linen, the fitness of personal behaviour, the quality of the liturgy, the excellence of the music, the care taken by the readers: all such things are positive aids to communion with God.

Finally to that list I will add one injunction put in homely language: 'do your homework!' You understand what I mean well enough, and I hope that this very talk of mine today has given a modest example of it. Read about your religion; keep yourself abreast of what the best theologians are writing and saying; penetrate as far as you can into the meaning of your liturgies; above all, throw yourself back in time to understand why we are where we are; read not only the Bible but St Augustine, Bede, St Aquinas, Cardinal Newman, de Chardin. Remember that, to use John Donne's words written nearly four hundred years ago, 'no man is an Island, entire of itself.'

Earlier, I read one of the gorgeous daily collects of the Book of Common Prayer and I end with another – the second collect of Morning Prayer, the prayer for peace in all its various forms. I shall read it fairly slowly, because as you savour its splendid and exquisitely balanced phrases, I would like you to try to discern the many interpretations of which it is susceptible. I need not tell you which version I shall use! Will you stand?

O God, who art the author of peace and lover of concord, in knowledge of whom standeth our eternal life, whose service is perfect freedom: Defend us thy humble servants in all assaults of our enemies; that we, surely trusting in thy defence, may not fear the power of any adversaries; through the might of Jesus Christ Our Lord. Amen.

The liturgy should be adapted to different circumstances, different moods. Intimacy and simplicity are proper to small groups. On other more formal occasions the emphasis should be on beauty, respect, awe, wonderment.

CARDINAL BASIL HUME

Stewardship in the great tradition
Cranmer and the continuing importance of the Book of Common Prayer in the spirituality of the Church of England[1]

PETER NEWMAN BROOKS

An Annual General meeting is an important occasion, and the speaker, even a stand-in speaker with Cambridge pressures upon him at Tripos time, is honoured by the invitation to address it, especially when consideration is given to the purpose of the Society. For you are – all of you, officers and members – a remarkable *ad hoc* body. Twenty years ago no one would have thought it conceivable that such a Society *would have to exist* and rally to the defence of a Liturgy that is as important to the Anglican tradition as St Paul's Cathedral. Indeed, it is as crucial to 'This royal throne of kings, this sceptred isle' as Westminster Abbey itself.

Yet here you are, possibly and understandably disheartened, yet emphatically dedicated to the great cause of preservation; and, this time, preservation not of some crumbling edifice, but of a living liturgy, a Book of Common Prayer, that you believe has captured Christian truth for our people, and by no means outlived its usefulness in our prayers and in our parishes.

If the bishops are against you, and 'lawful authority' either patronising or lukewarm in its attitude, you cannot be blamed for feeling abandoned. But let an historian emphasise that since the time of the Reformation itself bishops of the Church of England have never been famed for their intelligence. Nowadays, of course, it is urged that the Church needs pastoral men to lead it, and that scholarship is out. You do not have to scrutinise ecclesiastical appointments long to appreciate that. Or, indeed, the corollary that Synods at every level are populated with a new kind of being: the Church Politician. 'Such men are dangerous.' Their very Christian commitment is at times suspect, in so far as they have little or no understanding of their heritage in the Great Tradition.

For such reasons the historian in me is thankful to God for the Prayer Book Society; and in the few moments you have allotted me this afternoon I want to encourage your stewardship in a noble cause. The priest ordained in the English Church is given 'Authority

to preach the Word of God', and, conscious of that responsibility
this afternoon, I wish to leave with you a message of consolation
and hope from the writings of the first Christian historian, St Luke.
'He that is faithful in that which is least, is faithful also in much'
(Luke 16:10). Although I am well aware that the story of the Unjust
Steward is fraught with difficulties of exegesis, it nevertheless seems
to me to symbolise the dilemma your Society faces in the contemporary Church (advocating, if you like, a little worldliness of the
kind that will help you to outwit those determined to dilute the
deposit of your faith and heritage). And it also focuses in microcosm
precisely the macrocosm of the Great Tradition, the rich heritage of
the Church of God. The present 'new lamps for old' approach
simply will not do, militating as it does against the inherited spirituality of the English people. For make no mistake about it, the
Book of Common Prayer is a very holy thing. To shelve it altogether,
as if it were some kind of embarrassing report of a select committee
of inquiry, would be as absurd as it would be to shelve Holy
Scripture itself, to abandon the very quarry, the bed-rock, whence
the liturgy was itself originally hewn. No, the English liturgy of
1662 must always remain an alternative to any new collection. And
it must be a real alternative – not some kind of compromise in the
tradition of the imagined *via media Anglicana*, or a mere early-
morning alternative celebrated in a side chapel. Heed some words
of John Henry Newman on the subject of such a compromise, words
taken from his *Lectures on the Prophetical Office of the Church* (1837):

> The *via media* has never existed except on paper, it has never
> been reduced to practice: it is known, not positively but negatively
> in its differences from the rival creeds, not in its own properties
> . . . what is this but to fancy a road over the mountains and rivers
> which has never been cut?

Truly, the Catholic side of the Great Tradition will not support the
kind of compromise that leads to desuetude, that deprives whole
generations of the essence of spirituality in the English Church.

I cannot bring myself this afternoon to discuss the modern rites
themselves . . . *series* whatever! In the past – in my Lectures at
Cambridge, and in a Reformation Sermon, a brief extract of which
was published in the last number of *Faith and Heritage* – I have
been so tempted, but set aside that temptation as unprofessional
polemic. We can all play to the gallery and imagine the reincarnation
of a Cranmer, furtive and ghostlike, inserting a new clause into his
ancient Litany that would catch the unwary: 'From the Dean of
York, and all his detestable enormities: *Good Lord, deliver us.*' We

can all wonder at the curious membership of the Liturgical Commission itself, marvelling at the 'lightness' of its scholarship, and its failure to appreciate the many-sidedness of the Great Tradition. But such topics are beyond the scope of public communication, and, possibly, at this stage of disillusionment, subjects only for private prayer – even for that beating of the breast and weeping that John Calvin advocated when the Church went sadly astray.

No, it is not part of my present purpose to add to the controversy. Rather do I stand before you this afternoon as a Cambridge don and Church historian, convinced that any serious attempt on the part of our bishops and 'church politicians' to by-pass the Book of Common Prayer is absolute folly. It would amount to cutting off our own roots as an historic Church and living household of faith. It has already frustrated many, many people in the parishes. When bishops thus bully their clergy to speed up experimentation, and the faithful in the parishes feel like resisting their priests, it is not pastoral care but *chaos* that results. Timid clergy are often fearful of ignoring episcopal directives; and ambitious clergy (of whom there are far too many nowadays) are so eager to press ahead that they invariably bruise the tender consciences of their people. Pastoral care? I fear not; for, either way, the result reflects a lack of concern and a curious craving for dull uniformity based on a kind of law-and-order theology that is far from the spirituality that should possess us all in the Great Tradition.

Frankly, the present situation affords great amusement to our critics, who look on as our leaders merely patronise the age in which we live. Many thus believe the Church of England to be in the hands of misguided modernists prepared to pawn the past with a lack of concern that knows nothing of pastoral priorities. In my brief life-span, the English Church sold out its schools to the State, whereas Rome chose rather to strengthen its specifically Christian cause in education. Very recently indeed, some of our most significant theological Colleges have been closed or amalgamated. And now the Prayer Book itself is under threat. What is *pastoral* here? Ecumenical considerations notwithstanding, faithful people and their spiritual overseers need to remain loyal to their heritage, to grasp afresh the freedom and abiding spirituality of the Great Tradition. To parody some words of Cranmer in his *Sermon on Rebellion*:

> Shall we now destroy our *Church* ['Realm' in the original], and make it a prey to our adversaries? Remember the fable of Aesop, that when the frog and the mouse did fight together, the puttock came, and snatched them up both.[2]

No good can come of such a situation; and it does not surprise the mere historian that the Church of England but rarely makes the headlines nowadays. The BBC's Religious Affairs correspondent, Gerald Priestland, made much of this point in his broadcast column very recently, observing that the pronouncements of a certain Cardinal Archbishop who, they tell me, lives not far from here, are far more newsworthy to the nation at large. And Priestland, you will recall, based it all on the spirituality of the man. Much the same argument could find a base in learning, the learning which nowadays our leaders not merely lack but increasingly scorn.

If they could any longer read the Latin tongue, many bishops might profit from a glance at Canon 10 of the *Reformatio Legum Ecclesiasticarum*, that remarkable attempt made in 1553 to reform the canon law of the English Church. It was composed by a committee that seated scholars like Thomas Cranmer and Peter Martyr round its table, and I quote the Canon *De Episcoporum gradu ac dignitate in Ecclesia*, concerning the Position and Dignity of Bishops in the Church:

> Bishops, because they hold the principal place . . . shall govern and have pastoral care for the lower orders of clergy and all God's people, with sound doctrine, weight of authority, and especially prudent counsel. They shall not, indeed, play the master over them, but show themselves to be truly the servants, of the servants, of God.
>
> Let them be aware that their ecclesiastical authority . . . is entrusted to them for no other reason than that by their ministry and diligence very many men may be united to Christ. Likewise, those who are already Christ's may thus thrive and come to maturity . . .[3]

What wisdom there is in such a context of pastoral concern! For make no mistake about it, stewardship in this vital matter of the Book of Common Prayer primarily relates to matters of the heart and soul. It is certainly for such considerations that Cranmer's masterpiece remains of the greatest comfort, providing consolation and hope today just as it has done down the long corridors of time.

In his liturgical worship, Cranmer was no mere philologist in the attention he gave his English prose, for the Archbishop was committed in full to both the New Divinity of Christian Humanism, and the pastoral inspiration of the Protestant Reformation of the sixteenth century. Albeit a man of his times, he clearly set his face against the total abandonment of the mediaeval tradition. His was, to be sure, the Pauline approach: 'Prove all things; hold fast that which is good.' (I Thess. 5:21)

It was a key principle that modifying the Mass put new life into the ancient *Sarum Use* and did duty as Cranmer laboured with dedication 'to turn the Mass into a Communion'. His was a properly *pastoral* concern: the root cause, let me emphasise once again, of the Reformation of the sixteenth century – analysed as possibly the greatest crisis in Christendom before the coming of the 1978 Reith Lecturer, Dr Edward Norman!

I promised to be serious – and as I conclude I would return to the theme of stewardship in terms of the Book of Common Prayer. For, basing his services on scriptural insight, Cranmer always strove to achieve simplicity. It was, moreover, a simplicity grounded in charitable supposition – that indefinable but essential ingredient of leaven in the lump of liturgy. His genius for communication likewise encompassed an economy of expression; and, by such means, his service of Holy Communion may be said to have refined the molasses of the Mass. Furthermore, in Cranmer's composition – committee authorship notwithstanding – there was the kind of agreeable charity that, while continuing the Great Tradition, conveyed neither fury nor fervour in many great and enduring prayers. For his was supremely the moderating influence of eirenicism.

The historical appeal of such a masterpiece has always been wide-spread, and in no way because Cranmer sought either ambiguity or compromise. Such accusations stem from the hostile witness of critics with little grasp of sixteenth-century Court intrigue. How apt, once again, is the *parallel* with the Unjust Steward. By contrast, Cranmer strove to perfect a doctrine of 'True and Spiritual' Presence in the Sacrament; and in so doing effectively antedated the realisation of Charles Simeon that 'Truth lies not in the middle, and not in one extreme, but in both extremes.'[4]

What balance, what wholeness is here. There are collects – the collect for Ascension Day provides a good example – that still the mind as gems of abiding spirituality:

> Grant, we beseech thee, Almighty God, that like as we do believe thy only-begotten Son our Lord Jesus Christ to have ascended into the heavens; so we may also in heart and mind thither ascend, and with him continually dwell. . .

There is that telescoping of the monastic offices which, particularly in terms of Evening Prayer, has long been the envy of Roman Christendom – not to mention its value as a focus of Psalm-singing revered the world over in BBC broadcasts of Choral Evensong. And above all, there is the hallowed ground of a Eucharist that has long been a pilgrimage shrine for the faithful of the English Church, whatever their actual background or precise placing in the Great Tradition.

Truly, my Lords, ladies and gentlemen, the work of the Lord Himself is here. So when, shortly, we proceed inside the Abbey Church of Westminster, where, on 30 March 1533, he was consecrated, let us have this same Thomas Cranmer in thankful remembrance, especially seeking, after him, to take our places as Stewards in the Great Tradition, serving those who would worship the Lord in the beauty of holiness – a holiness that, thanks be to God, does not fade. Amen.

References

1 An address to the Annual General Meeting of the Prayer Book Society, held in the Jerusalem Chamber of Westminster Abbey, 2 June 1979.
2 J. E. Cox (ed.), *Miscellaneous Writings and Letters of Thomas Cranmer* (Parker Society, 1846), p 193.
3 E. Cardwell (ed.), *The Reformation of the Ecclesiastical Laws. . .* (1850), pp 103–4.
4 Quoted in Gordon Rupp, *Protestant Catholicity* (1960), p 40.

The other liturgical revolution

I. R. THOMPSON

Ever since Series 3 made its controversial appearance, attention has focused on the language of the new rites. Liturgical revision, it seemed, was about what we *say* and *hear* when we attend a church service; hardly anyone (among the traditionalists) called attention to the fact that it is also about what we *see* and *do*. The publication, separately and at intervals, of the full range of Series 3 services, discussion about the proposed Alternative Service Book, and debates in Parliament and in the national press about the availability of the Prayer Book, have all contributed to this one-sided emphasis on textual revision. And all the while another and less official form of liturgical revision – one that has nothing to do with books or booklets – has been quietly gathering pace. It may be seen in the now widespread tendency of clergy to celebrate westward, facing the people; in the extraordinary growth and diversity of congregational participation; in the practice of standing instead of kneeling to receive communion, and in the less common (but growing) practice whereby communicants administer the sacrament to one another; in the reordering of church interiors, etc.

It is customary to explain these changes in terms of the new emphasis on the *corporate* nature of public worship, but there is more to it than just this. The new stagecraft (if I may invoke a term to cover all the innovations which I am concerned with here) is the outcome of a profound revolution in academic circles, the aim of which is to re-educate worshippers into a totally new understanding of terms like 'church' and 'worship'. It is no longer Prayer Book language or even Prayer Book theology that is the main target of the liturgical radicals: it is the traditional concept of the sacred itself.

Consider, for example, the changing attitude to churches as consecrated buildings.

The classic statement of the Anglican position on this matter is to be found in Hooker.[1] Churches are places set apart for holy use; hence their dedication: 'It notifieth in solemn manner the holy and religious use whereunto it is intended such houses shall be put.' Moreover to dedicate a church is 'to surrender up that right which otherwise their founders might have in them, and to make God

Himself their owner.' Of course, true worship is true worship wherever it is offered. Nevertheless church buildings are – or at any rate can be – considerable aids to devotion, and that which is set apart for God's use ought not to be profaned. 'The argument which our Saviour useth against profaners of the temple (Matt. 21:13), he taketh from the use whereunto it was with solemnity consecrated.' Hooker nowhere implies that churches must be splendid buildings; obviously economic factors operate here. But he evidently recognises an important distinction between the sacred and the secular. 'Christ could not suffer that the temple should serve for a place of mart, nor the Apostle of Christ that the church should be made an inn' – a reference to 1 Cor. 11:22.

This, as I say, is the 'classic' Anglican statement of the matter and there seems little reason to doubt that it is still the attitude of the vast majority of ordinary churchgoers. But it is an attitude which is coming increasingly under attack. Only last year, for example, the University of Birmingham Institute for the Study of Worship and Religious Architecture published a collection of essays entitled *The Recreational Use of Churches*, hoping thereby to stimulate discussion on ways in which churches still used for worship may be brought to serve the needs of the wider community. In a chapter entitled 'The Adaptation of Church Buildings', Martin Purdy draws our attention to the fact that 'latterly there has been a decline in formal religious observance' (one wonders just what informal religious observances he has in mind) and then goes on to argue (pp 20–22) that sport and recreation constitute 'a growing need'. The chapter is generously illustrated with drawings and diagrams showing how churches may be partitioned to create squash courts, billiard rooms and coffee bars as well as 'free space for worship, games, concerts, etc.' Professor J. G. Davies, the Director of the Institute, and an enthusiastic disciple of the new thinking, even contributes a section on the history of games in churches – a curious catalogue of bygone profanities such as dicing, skittles, various kinds of 'good humoured buffoonery', semi-pagan festivals (maypoles could be and were erected in churches), ball games, wrestling, acrobatics and the like. Of course many of these activities were strenuously opposed by the ecclesiastical authorities, but Professor Davies encourages his readers to view them more indulgently. 'On occasion . . . they [the bishops] were right to condemn excesses; frequently they were wrong in trying to separate the things of God from everyday activities such as recreation, for without the creative and sustaining activity of God, so Christians believe, there could not be any everyday.' He concedes that some activities were indeed unsavoury, like the bear-baiting that took place in Woburn church in 1612 and the cock-fighting around the communion table in the 1630s at Knottingley. But he begs the reader to observe the basis of his objection. 'It is not because these activities took place in a church that I regard them as wrong: they are wrong on moral grounds *wherever they may be indulged in,*' (p 18). Clearly Professor Davies is anxious to challenge the whole principle of consecration – i.e., the setting apart of things for religious purposes. 'God', he argues, 'is to be found in the midst of life or not at all.'

Now this idea – that God is to be encountered in the commonplace – was the central feature of a well-known book of the 60s; a book, moreover, which continues to exercise an enormous influence on liturgical thinking. I refer, of course, to John Robinson's *Honest to God*.

In the chapter entitled 'Worldly Holiness' Robinson argues for an end to 'churchiness and religiosity and everything that sets apart the sanctuary from society'. He would like to see 'the décor, the music and the architecture speak the language of the world it is meant to be transforming'. One may note, in passing, the origin here of much of the current hostility to the Prayer Book, for whether or not the Prayer Book remains intelligible to ordinary churchgoers, and whatever its literary merits, clearly it does not speak the language of everyday life. But Robinson is more concerned in this chapter with what I referred to as the 'stagecraft' of worship.

> The so-called 'eastward position', in which the priest stands with his back to the people, has the psychological effect of focusing attention upon a point somewhere in the middle distance beyond the sanctuary. It symbolises the whole way of thinking in which God is seen as a projection 'out there' to whom we turn from the world. By contrast the 'westward position' in which the president[2] surrounded by his assistants faces the people across the table, focuses attention upon a point in the middle, as the Christ stands amongst his own as the breaker of bread.

The westward position also has the effect – and evidently a very desirable one to Bishop Robinson's way of thinking – of helping to remove from the communion service the element of *personal* devotion:

> Too often . . . it [i.e. the Eucharist] ceases to be a holy meal, and becomes a religious service in which we turn our backs on the common and the community and in individualistic devotion go to 'make our communion' with 'the God out there'. This is the

essence of the religious perversion, when worship becomes a realm into which to withdraw from the world to 'be with God' – even if it is only in order to receive strength to go back into it. In this case the entire realm of the non-religious (in other words, 'life' [*sic*]) is relegated to the profane, in the strict sense of that which is outside the *fanum* or sanctuary. The holy place, where the Christ is met, lies not, as in the parable of the Sheep and the Goats, in the ordinary relationships of life: it lies within the circle of 'the religious'; from which the worshipper will go out to carry Christ's love into 'the secular world'. Worship, liturgy, on this understanding, is not meeting the holy *in* the common. The holy is that which is not common and which has to be taken from the temple in order to sanctify the common.

One can trace back to this and similar passages, much of the contemporary urge to get worship 'out of the churches' and, what is the next best thing, to reorder the interior of churches so that they take on a reassuringly 'secular' look. In speaking of the sanctuary, Robinson is, of course, referring to the church building as a whole, but the very idea of an internal sanctuary – a region at the east end of the church fenced in by communion rails and containing the communion table – runs counter to everything he says. For the sanctuary is a most powerful symbol of the old way of thinking: a visual reminder that the sacred is the protected, the inviolable, the apart.

Hence the revolution in liturgical stagecraft. If people can be taught to communicate standing, communion rails can be dispensed with; and if communion rails can be dispensed with (and even sometimes if they can't) the communion table can be removed to a more central position in the body of the church. Here indeed is Robinson's ideal of the Christian assembly: the gathering around, instead of in linear fashion, so that Christ may be more obviously 'in the midst'. But once you subscribe to this way of thinking where do you stop? If it is wrong to make a distinction between the sacred and the secular, can it possibly be right to make a distinction between priest and people? For the ordained minister is, by virtue of his calling, his ordination and his special function on liturgical occasions, a literal embodiment of that which is 'set apart'. There are grounds for thinking that the crisis of identity which seems to be afflicting many of the clergy at the moment – particularly apparent in a tendency to denigrate their own ministerial function – owes at least something to the influence of books like *Honest to God*. And here we may notice yet another feature of the new stagecraft – i.e.

the practice of encouraging (or requiring) communicants to administer the sacrament to one another.[3] For in this way (a) the priestly
role is reduced to a bare minimum; and (b) the individual relationship between priest and communicant – so pregnant with overtones
of a personal communion – ceases to exist. Here, if anywhere, is
the liturgical expression of the idea that God is to be encountered
in the midst of life or not at all.

What is one to make of all this? Can it be true that we need to
reorientate our thinking along the lines suggested by the radicals?
Is it really perverse to want to withdraw from the world, even if
only for a short time, in order 'to be with God'? These are questions
which merit more detailed treatment than they can possibly receive
here or at my hands; and yet I cannot leave this subject without
saying why I believe the new thinking to be wrong.

And first with regard to the curious notion that personal (or as
Bishop Robinson prefers to call it, 'individualistic') devotion has no
place at the Eucharist. I call it a curious notion because it is not
easy to see how personal devotion *can* be eliminated from a consideration of our Lord's atoning sacrifice. I am not suggesting that
the individual is not redeemed in and through the Church Universal.
Nevertheless, he is redeemed because he is forgiven; and the offer
of forgiveness demands a personal response. I know it is fashionable
to argue that personal devotion was not a feature of the primitive
Eucharist but those who propound this theory would seem to be
confusing two quite different things. It may be true that prior to
the fourth century there was little, if anything, in the nature of
'communion devotions' (i.e., special prayers in preparation for the
individual act of receiving communion); but to suggest that the
primitive Eucharist did not invite, and produce, an intensity of
personal feeling, is to fly in the face of almost all the evidence we
possess. Take the following passage, for example, from a letter
written by St Ignatius of Antioch, shortly before his martyrdom *c.*
AD 112:

> I am alive at this writing, but my desire is to die. My love is
> crucified, and I have no secular fire left: but there is in me living
> water, speaking to me within, and saying, Come to the Father.
> I delight not in corruptible food, nor in the entertainments of this
> world. The bread of God is what I covet; heavenly bread, bread
> of life, namely the flesh of Christ Jesus the Son of God, who in
> these last times became the Son of David and of Abraham: and

I am athirst for the drink of God, namely his blood, which is a feast that faileth not, and life everlasting. I have no desire to live any longer among men; neither shall I, if you will but consent.[4]

The reader may judge for himself whether this passage is closer in spirit to the traditional or to the modern teaching on the Eucharist and also whether it lends any support to Bishop Robinson's views on withdrawal from the world. All I would ask him to remember is its very early date.

There is, in any case, much more that could be said on the question of 'withdrawing apart'. Did not our Lord commend the contemplative Mary above the practical Martha? Was he not himself in the habit of withdrawing apart into a mountain to pray? We may acknowledge that for the Christian, 'life' involves belonging to a community but, as St John never tires of reminding us, the Christian community is not the world! Nor is the church any ordinary community, being, in the words of the Prayer Book, 'the blessed company of all faithful people' wherever they may be. Thus

> Even the anchorite who meditates alone,
> For whom the days and nights repeat the praise of GOD,
> Prays for the church, the Body of Christ incarnate.
>
> T. S. ELIOT

And thus the Church has always insisted that the anchorite is no less a Christian because he dwells and prays (in one sense) alone. The clause 'I believe in the Communion of Saints' would be superfluous if it referred only to that which can be demonstrated by overt acts. The whole point of an article of faith is that it calls attention to a mystical reality which cannot be demonstrated or observed. It may be that, in its gentler manifestations,[5] the new stagecraft makes us more conscious of the *human* aspects of Christian fellowship; but if it tends to obscure the *mystical* aspects (and there are many who would claim that it does precisely that), then the loss surely outweighs the gain.

This brings me to some of the wider issues raised by the new thinking. For if it is wrong to make a distinction between the sacred and the secular what becomes of the traditional antithesis between the Church and the world? There is no doubt that to the early Christians the Church was pre-eminently the manifestation of the holy on earth. It was 'new Jerusalem', 'holy and without blemish', especially to be differentiated from the fallen creation into which men are born. We tend to forget nowadays that this concept was given liturgical expression in the refusal of the primitive Church to allow unbaptised persons even to witness the Eucharist. Here emphatically was the equation: the holy = the apart! Moreover if the holy is not, in at least some of its manifestations, 'that which has to be taken from the temple in order to sanctify the common', how do we explain the concept of sacramental grace? Robinson skates uneasily round this problem by arguing that the bread used at the Eucharist should be, to quote the words of the Prayer Book, 'such as is usual to be eaten'. And so it perhaps ought to be. Nevertheless, by the prayer of the Church and the power of the Holy Spirit, it becomes sanctified bread, different in effect from what it was before. The new thinking at least de-emphasises this point and in fact begets a tendency to deny what the sacraments exist to assert: namely the moral and spiritual *insufficiency* of the natural order of things. If the sacred and the secular are already indissolubly associated, there is no need for any special infusion of holiness; no need for sacraments as we commonly understand them; nor does man stand in need of that special activity of the divine goodness which we call sanctifying grace.

One further point. Man's knowledge of the sacred is not purely doctrinal or theoretical. It is both instinctive (as when, for example, at especially solemn moments we tend to speak in hushed voices) and also – for some people – the result of direct (i.e., mystical) experience. I am obliged to say something about the latter if only because there is a school of thought, prominently represented by the writings of Teilhard de Chardin, which adduces certain forms of mystical experience to support the contention that the sacred and the secular are 'organically' united – i.e., that they are merely two ways of looking at God's one world. Now undoubtedly it is given to certain individuals to see material things, as it were, transfigured and spiritualised; as embodying a life-force which may be described as supra-normal. We may recall the poet Wordsworth's description of his childhood as

> . . . a time when meadow, grove and stream,
> The earth, and every common sight,
> To me did seem
> Apparelled in celestial light,
> The glory and the freshness of a dream.
>
> 'Ode on Intimations of Immortality'

Nevertheless we must beware of reading into such experiences an interpretation which they will not bear. True, the mystic tends to see 'the holy in the common', but he also knows that the common is not universally holy. There is the world of the vision, and there is the stubborn, residual world which the vision fails to embrace. If nature can be 'personal' and holy, it can also be impersonal and savage (it was, after all, the deeply mystical Tennyson who coined the phrase, 'Nature, red in tooth and claw'). In particular, man himself is seen to be out of harmony with the divine impulse. It was no sour cleric but again the poet Wordsworth who penned that memorable and bitter protest:

> If this belief from heaven be sent,
> If such be Nature's holy plan,
> Have I not reason to lament
> What man has made of man?
>
> 'Lines written in early spring'

It also needs to be observed that there is about mystical experience *a sense of that which is not common currency;* of that, which, because it is holy, must be respected and guarded. I can perhaps best illustrate what I mean by referring to a well-known short story by H. G. Wells, The Door in the Wall, about a boy who discovered an enchanted garden. Being really quite young, and being obsessed with his discovery, he told his secret to a group of scoffing school-mates. Even as he did so he had a feeling that 'in some way it was against the rules'. The brief popularity which his disclosure brought him was at the expense of a 'secret self disgust . . . a really painful undertow of shame at telling what I felt was indeed a *sacred secret*'. Significantly, when he tried to show his companions the entrance to the enchanted garden, it could not be found.

Now the sense of the holy as that which so easily can, but at all costs must not, be violated or profaned, is one of the most striking features of authentic religious experience (think of St Paul's remark in 2 Cor. 12:4, that he had heard 'unspeakable words, *which it is not lawful for a man to utter*'. It is also, of course, a feature of the quasi-religious experience of being in love. As Charles Dickens observed, in the words of one of his characters:

> I hazard the guess that the true lover's mind is completely per-meated by the beloved object of his affections. I hazard the guess that her dear name is precious to him, cannot be heard or repeated without emotion, and is preserved sacred. If he has any distin-guishing appellation of fondness for her, it is reserved for her, and it is not for common ears. A name that it would be a privilege to call her by, being alone with her own bright self, it would be a liberty, a coldness, an insensibility, almost a breach of good

faith, to flaunt elsewhere.

The Mystery of Edwin Drood, Chapter 11.

If man is to be true to his religious vision then he must, I submit, be prepared to acknowledge, and give expression to, the essential apartness, the not-to-be-violated quality of the sacred. If the language, the setting and the performance of the liturgy do not engender this sense of apartness, then the mystery is lost, and worship ceases to be worship in the fullest sense of the word. Worse, it may actually give pain and offence to the worshipper by violating what he feels to be some of the essential qualities of the sacred. Worst of all it may (in the long term) diminish or actually destroy our conscious understanding of the sacred itself.

References

1 Richard Hooker, *Of the Laws of Ecclesiastical Politie* (1594–7), v. 12.
2 Note the use of the term 'president'. This was in 1962: almost a decade before the genesis of Series 3.
3 This represents a clear break with the universal custom of the Church in all ages. In the primitive Church, communion was administered either by the deacons (see Justin Martyr's *Apology*, i. 65) or by a combination of bishop/presbyter and deacon (rubrics of the fourth-century *Liturgy of the Apostolic Constitutions*). Tertullian, writing about AD 200 states, 'the sacrament of the eucharist we receive . . . from the hands of no others than the heads of the Church' (*De Corona, iii*).
4 *Epistle to the Romans* 7. In similar vein, St Clement of Alexandria talks of partaking 'of the new food of Christ, receiving him, if possible, so as to lay him up within ourselves and to inclose our Saviour in our breasts' (*Paedag.* i.6).
5 Some of its manifestations are embarrassingly forceful – what Professor David Martin calls 'mandatory communalism'. He observes that 'Christians are now enjoined to stand, literally in a circle, backs to the world, each exposed to the inquisition of other eyes. The defensible space of individuality is eroded. Some like it, and expansively adopt the 'Kiss of Peace', while others feel grossly intruded upon, unable to frame their petitions to Almighty God. The Church exudes groupiness and generates a kind of eucharistic MRA. . . .' (*PN Review* 13).

Notes on the contributors
Acknowledgments

Notes on the contributors

Sydney Carter, poet, song-writer and performer, born 1915. He is probably best known for 'Lord of the Dance', which is now included in many hymn books. His publications include *The Two Way Clock* (poems), *Green Print for Song*, *In the present tense* (songs) and *The Rock of Doubt* (prose and graffiti).

Andor Gomme, Reader in English at the University of Keele. By inclination a private person, but he has written books of architectural history. Currently of no fixed religious abode.

Peggy Makins, journalist and broadcaster. For many years she had a column in *Woman* magazine and under the name of Evelyn Home answered readers' personal problems. On retirement she became a member of the Central Religious Advisory Committee, and a counsellor on late night BBC radio programmes. She contributes to the BBC's 'Thought for the day', 'Prayer for the day', and the Overseas feature, 'Reflections'. Peggy Makins belongs to the Society of Friends.

David Martin, Professor of Sociology at the London School of Economics, born 1929. President of the International Conference of the Sociology of Religions; Cadbury Lecturer (Birmingham); Ferguson Lecturer (Manchester); Lecturer in Pastoral Theology (Durham); Gore Lecturer (Westminster Abbey); JSPS Scholar (Japan); Firth Lecturer (Nottingham); Select Preacher, Cambridge University (1979). Author of several books on contemporary religious problems. David Martin is particularly interested in Handel's music and a lover of church music.

Brian Morris, Professor of English Literature at the University of Sheffield, and General Editor of the New Arden Shakespeare and the New Mermaid series. He has published two collections of poems, *Tide Race* and *Stones in the Brook*, and a third volume is forthcoming. He is a member of the Standing Commission on Museums and Galleries, a Trustee of the National Portrait Gallery, a member of the Welsh Arts Council Literature Committee, and appears regularly in BBC radio and television programes.

A. L. Rowse has made equal contributions to literature and history, with several volumes of autobiography, seven of poetry, and collections of essays. His historical work has been mainly on the Elizabethan age, on which he is a leading authority, with his classic trilogy on the Elizabethan Renaissance and his work on Shakespeare. This led him to the solution of the problems of the Sonnets and identification of the Dark Lady. His latest books are *A Man of the Thirties*, described by the *Sunday Times* as 'a classic of modern autobiography', and *Portraits and Views*, mainly literary.

Fraser Steel was born in Scotland in 1950, and educated at Manchester Grammar School and Pembroke College, Cambridge. In 1973 he joined the BBC as a producer of radio talks and documentaries. At present based in Manchester, he is responsible for poetry broadcasting on Radio 3 and 4. He sings (Cantoris tenor, and occasional precentor) with the choir of St Peter's, Prestbury.

Gordon Taylor, Rector of St Giles-in-the-Fields, London WC2, since 1949, writes from long practical experience in the pastoral ministry. As a naval chaplain his war service at sea in destroyers, armed merchant cruisers and the battleship, HMS *Rodney*, particularly brought him into contact with the common man's religious problems. He is the author of *The Sea Chaplains*, a definitive history recently published. At St Giles-in-the-Fields he introduced a lunchtime ministry for city workers, and an annual Bible School, conducted by visiting Bible scholars, which since 1971 has achieved 10,000 attendances.

Ian Thompson, Head of the English Department at Frederick Gough Comprehensive School, Scunthorpe. He is a member of the General Synod of the Church of England and editor of *Faith and Worship*, a half-yearly review published by the Prayer Book Society.

Bryan Thwaites is a mathematician by training and profession, and has done such varied things as being a schoolmaster, a professor, a Past President of the Institute of Mathematics and its Application, and the founder of the School Mathematics project. But as a lifelong and committed Anglican (married to a Roman Catholic) he has tried to incorporate into all his educational activities a sense of Christian purpose and commitment. He has been Principal of Westfield College since 1966, and is particularly proud of the fact that under his guidance the College retained in its new charter and statutes the requirement that the work of the College should be conducted according to Christian principles.

J. P. Ward, Lecturer in the sociology of education at University College, Swansea, has Degrees in Classics, English and Sociology from the universities of Toronto, Cambridge and Wales. Since 1975 he has been editor of *Poetry Wales*, and has published two books of poetry, one of concrete poetry, and a monograph on the education of adolescent girls. He has contributed poetry and criticism to *Encounter*, *The Listener* and other journals.

Acknowledgments

Grateful acknowledgment is made for permission to quote the following copyright material:

André Deutsch Ltd for lines from 'The Pentecost Castle' by Geoffrey Hill published in *Tenenbrae*; Faber Ltd for lines from the poetry of W. H. Auden and T. S. Eliot; David Higham Associates Ltd for an extract from *Akenfield* by Ronald Blythe, published by Allen Lane and Penguin Ltd; and for 'On being asked to write a school hymn' by Charles Causley, from his *Collected Poems* published by Macmillan Ltd; SCM Press Ltd for extracts from *Honest to God* by John Robinson; and the Literary Executors of Stevie Smith for the poem 'Why are the clergy . . . ?' from *Not Waving But Drowning* published by André Deutsch Ltd.